James Ferguson

Two Scottish Soldiers

A soldier of 1688 and Blenheim, a soldier of the American revolution, and a

Jacobite laird and his forbears

James Ferguson

Two Scottish Soldiers

A soldier of 1688 and Blenheim, a soldier of the American revolution, and a Jacobite laird and his forbears

ISBN/EAN: 9783337006624

Printed in Europe, USA, Canada, Australia, Japan

Cover: Foto ©ninafisch / pixelio.de

More available books at **www.hansebooks.com**

TWO SCOTTISH SOLDIERS

AND

A JACOBITE LAIRD.

TWO SCOTTISH SOLDIERS

A SOLDIER OF 1688 AND BLENHEIM

A SOLDIER OF THE AMERICAN REVOLUTION

AND

A JACOBITE LAIRD AND HIS FORBEARS

BY

JAMES FERGUSON

ABERDEEN: D. WYLLIE & SON
1888

Adelphi Press, Aberdeen:
TAYLOR AND HENDERSON,
PRINTERS TO THE QUEEN.

CONTENTS.

I.

BRIGADIER FERGUSON, A SOLDIER OF 1688 AND BLENHEIM—

(1.) IN THE SCOTS BRIGADE.
(2.) COLONEL OF THE CAMERONIANS.
(3.) BRIGADIER AT BLENHEIM.

PAGE.

(1.) Parentage of Brigadier Ferguson—The "Scots Brigade"—In England for Monmouth's Rebellion—Lands with William of Orange at Torbay—Serves in Scottish Campaign—Taken prisoner at Killiecrankie—Commands expedition to Western Islands, commences building of Fort-William, and fights action in Mull—Given freedom of Glasgow and Edinburgh—Transferred to the Cameronian regiment after Steinkirk 1

(2.) The Cameronians—Obtains command after Landen—Service with the regiment in Dutch pay—In Scotland—First marriage—Papers illustrating history of the regiment—Letter to Principal Carstares—Incident with Lord Lovat at Bois-le-Duc 18

(2.) Ferguson's Brigade assembles at Bois-le-Duc, and temporarily takes over Maestricht from the Dutch—Arrival of Marlborough—The Brigadier's will—The storm of the lines of Schellenberg—Battle of Blenheim—Ferguson's brigade attacks the village—List of casualties and Muster-Rolls of the Cameronian regiment—Detached with the French prisoners to Holland—Second marriage—Campaign of 1705—Sudden death—Letter from Duke of Marlborough 31

II.

LIEUTENANT-COLONEL PATRICK FERGUSON, A SOLDIER OF THE AMERICAN REVOLUTION.

(1.) THE FIRST BREECHLOADING RIFLE.
(2.) THE "BATTLE SUMMER" OF 1780.
(3.) KING'S MOUNTAIN.

(1.) Parentage of Colonel P. Ferguson—Biography by Adam Ferguson, LL.D.—Tone of American references—"Old Minorca's" care—

viii.

PAGE.

With the Scots Grey in Germany—Gallantry—Duel with French swordsman at Paris—Writes on the Scotch Militia question—In the West Indies with the 70th regiment—Invents and takes out patent for Breechloading Rifle—Experiments with the new arm before the King—Volunteers for service in America—Obtains command of picked corps of riflemen—Commended for "spirited conduct" at battle of Brandywine—Incident with General Washington—Ferguson's account of it—American notices—Severely wounded—Commands successful expedition against Little Egg Harbour—Surprises Pulaski's legion—His "spirited service"—The "inoffending Quakers"—Employed on fortifications at Stoneypoint ... 55

(2.) Phase of American struggle in 1780—Ferguson's corps cover advance into South Carolina—Affair at Macpherson's Plantation—Wounded—His "sharpshooters"—Storms redoubt at Charleston—Covers the siege—Surprise of Monk's Corner—Instance of humanity—Organisation of the province—Duties as administrator—Organises loyal militia—The "Battle Summer" of 1780—Importance of the operations in the Carolinas—Detached to the western districts—Personal incidents—Chesney's reminiscences—Defeats enemy at Ironworks—Fight on Broad River—Advances and encamps at Gilbert-town—Success—Dismisses loyalist cavalry and militia on furlough—Endeavours to intercept Clarke's American force—Gathering of the backwoodsmen—Approach of superior force—Issues address to loyalists—Falls back to King's Mountain—Reasons of his tactics 75

(3.) King's Mountain—Increase in numbers of Americans—Capture of cook—Activity of spies—The Americans press on—The loyalist position—The Americans attack—Loyalist bayonet charges—Bravery of the defenders—The Americans seven times repulsed—Fall of Colonel Ferguson—Surrender of the survivors—Importance of the reverse—Incidents of the fight—Slaughter after surrender—Details—Bravery and losses of the Provincials—The last charge—Local tradition—American tributes to the loyalist leader's conduct—Buried by neighbouring villagers—Sufferings of wounded—Relics of the battle—The "Tory tulip-tree"—Hanging of prisoners—Effect of the action upon the campaign—Accounts of the time—American despatches—Extracts from letters of Colonel Ferguson—Colonel Tarleton's reminiscences—Estimates of friends—Verses—Epitaph. 94

III.

A JACOBITE LAIRD AND HIS FORBEARS,

OR

THE FORBESES OF BLACKTON.

MS. Memorial addressed to Prince Charles Edward in 1745—The last Blackton—Principles of the family—The 7th Lord Forbes grants

PREFATORY NOTE.

THE first and the third of the following sketches were originally written for the writer's personal pleasure, or the amusement of a limited circle. It has been suggested that they may have a wider interest, as illustrating two distinct and well-defined types of Scottish character, and that, in the year 1888 in particular, there may be a special interest in following the steps of a soldier of 1688, who afforded a characteristic specimen of the men who made the Revolution possible in Scotland. If the evils of a long protracted and embittered civil war, repeating the "Iliad of Woes" experienced by the previous generation, were avoided, this result was due, in the first place, to the statesmanship with which William of Orange used the power at which he had struck so boldly; and, in the second place, to the firmness and fidelity with which he was served by those who had become attached to his leadership abroad. There is much to be said for Burke's contention that the Revolution of 1688 was wrongly so called, and that it was "a revolution prevented rather than a revolution effected," but it is at least certain that the proceedings and the policy which the landing at Torbay inaugurated were dominated, not by the spirit of anarchy and disturbance, but by the spirit of order and discipline. It was to this that the British Constitution owed its solidity and stability, and the same qualities may be traced in the individual lives of many whose efforts contributed in lesser degrees to the history of the nation.

If the soldier of 1688, to whose story a recent visit to Holland enabled some further details to be supplied, illustrates one pronounced type of Scottish character, the Jacobite Laird exhibits another in the "Memorial" which suggested the notice of himself "and his Forbears." Theirs was the spirit of chivalrous loyalty,

"Which still keeps true whate'er betide,
And for his sake flings a' beside."

and his simple and imperfectly expressed narrative brings vividly before us the privations of the frosty night on the slopes of the Ochils, the horrors of the Black Hole of Stirling Castle, and the dreaded shadow of "Carlisle Wa." In one way these two sketches present a contrast curiously complete. The commander of the Cameronians was an adherent of the Prince of Orange, in a northern family mainly of Jacobite sympathies; the Forbeses of Blackton were the Cavalier branch of a clan, conspicuous as the chief Covenanters of the North.

The second sketch may be considered as a companion picture to the first, as the one deals with a soldier's life during the British, and the other during the American Revolution. The appearance of an article upon Colonel Ferguson, and the breechloading rifle which he invented, in a magazine of 1882, added to the scanty British sources which had then been tapped, a large supply of information from America, indicating how much interest has been felt on the other side of the Atlantic in the operations in which he fell, and his breechloader disappeared. It was satisfactory to find that this fresh information, much of it from sources that would once have been called hostile, in no instance tarnished the good name, and frequently expressed in more glowing language the estimate already formed of the character of the Scottish soldier who lost his life in the endeavour "to cover a country in which there were so many well affected inhabitants."

I have to express my best thanks to M. Van der Does de Willebois, Burgomaster; and M. Hezenmanns, Archevist of Bois-le-Duc; to M. Hinkmann, of the Rijks Archief, the Hague; M. J. H. Ferguson, the Hague; Major-General J. Watts de Peyster, of Rosehill, Tivoli, Duchess County, N.Y., and 59 East 21st Street, New York; and other friends in Aberdeenshire and elsewhere, for assistance courteously afforded in tracing out details, and especially to General de Peyster for permission to reproduce the drawings of the breechloading rifle.

J. F.

KINMUNDY,
OLD DEER, *September*, 1888.

charter to his youngest son, Abraham, the 1st of Blackton—Submission between "the clan and name of Forbes and the hous of Drum Irvine"—James Forbes, 2nd of Blackton—Marries M. Fraser of Philorth—His brother, Arthur, present at the Trot of Turriff—An "expert and brave commander"—An "excommunicated malignant"—Another relative, John, in the Covenanter's army—The raid upon the chaplain-tutor—The Laird's sons sent to Douay—Meet Father Blackhall and Lady Henrietta Gordon—" Royally entertained"—*Uxorem duxit, et hocreticus factus est*—Arthur Forbes of Balvenie—Walter Forbes, 3rd of Blackton—Birth brieve of his sister, Jean Forbes—Marries a Forbes of Corsindae—Activity of the Presbytery of Turriff—" The unlawful engagement"—" Promise by letter"—" Employed in giving of a band for keeping of the peace of the country"—" Called and compeired not"—Ordained "to satisfie"—"And so the process to ceass"—Alexander Forbes, 4th of Blackton—Granted freedom of Elgin in 1687—Marries Isobel Hacket—William Forbes, 5th of Blackton—Serves in Flanders—Wounded at Bouchain—Marries, 1st, Jane Brodie of Muiresk—1715—Joins the Chevalier's army at Perth—Lieutenant in Lord Panmure's regiment—Taken prisoner at Sheriffmuir—Sufferings at Dunblane and Stirling—In Edinburgh Castle—At Carlisle—Account of the trials—Provost Hay of Perth—Stewart of Tannachy-Tulloch—Blacktons own experiences—The discharge—Interview with the Judges at the Vintner's house—The "sacred and heavy oath"—2nd marriage to Mary Cumine of Auchry—Sale of Blackton—The claim to Balvenie—1745—" Two very great impediments" to joining the Prince—The "somewhat sacred" oath—The lawsuit which had ruined him—" My sore antagonist"— The Court of Session—"Just Judges"—The Prince's "most sincere well-wisher to power"—Marriage of his grand-daughter in 1756—Death in 1771. 125

APPENDIX.

I. THE POSITION OF THE SCOTS BRIGADE IN HOLLAND	151
II. COMMISSIONS IN THE SCOTS BRIGADE	153
III. THE DRUMMONDS OF CULTMALINDIE ...	... 157
IV. LATIN POEM SENT TO PRINCIPAL CARSTARES	... 158
V. NOTE ON OLD LINEN	160
VI. LOSSES OF FERGUSON'S BRIGADE, 1704 ...	... 160
VII. CAPTAIN ABRAHAM DE PEYSTER'S CHALLENGE	... 161

ILLUSTRATIONS.

The Ferguson Rifle, reproduced from cuts taken from the original in the possession of Major-General J. Watts de Peyster, State of New York, U. S. A. - - - - FRONTISPIECE.

Major-General James Ferguson of Balmakelly - - TO FACE ARTICLE I.

Brigadier Ferguson's Gorget - - - - - - - PAGE 52

Lieut.-Colonel Patrick Ferguson - - - - - TO FACE PAGE 54

"The Tory Tulip-Tree," King's Mountain, South Carolina - PAGE 122

Arm Chair of William Forbes of Blackton - - - - PAGE 148

Arms of "Major James Ferguson in Colonell Lauder's Regiment" —Lyon Register, 1691 - - - - ON FACE OF COVER.

Arms on Snuff-Box, also stamped "William Forbes of Blacktown" - - - - - - - ON REVERSE OF COVER.

I.

BRIGADIER FERGUSON,

A Soldier of 1688 and Blenheim.

"*We have our good service to plead for us; and that we have been honest and loyal from the beginning, and will continue so to the end.*"—LETTER OF BRIGADIER FERGUSON.

A SOLDIER OF 1688 AND BLENHEIM

I.

IN THE SCOTS BRIGADE.

"OH, Randal was a bonnie lad when he gaed awa—
A bonnie, bonnie lad was he, when he gaed awa !
It was in the Saxteen Hunner year o' grace and Thretty-twa,
That Randal, the laird's youngest son, gaed awa.
It was to seek his fortune in the Hie Germanie,
To fecht the foreign loons in their ain countrie,
That he left his father's ha' o' sweet Willanslee,
And mony sair hairts in the North Countrie."
—*Old Ballad.*

"HISTORY," it has been said, "is the essence of innumerable biographies," and the best way of judging a national movement often is to trace the career of a man. As there is always a deeper interest in politics, when to the stimulus of party and the inspiration of the great public cause is added the magic of the personality of a great leader, so in the narratives of the past we seem to see our way more clearly when subordinate events are allowed to group themselves around the achievements of some famous character who dominated the scene. It may be that in modern developments individuality is on the wane, yet the many works of fiction in which the author writes as an actor in the drama still pay a tribute to that human weakness which leads the student to place himself in the position of an eyewitness. But apart altogether from personal narratives, or the principal actors who tread the stage, something of the same feeling ever lends interest to the lives of those who acted even small parts in great events, and contributed what in them lay to the determination of important issues. The composed fortitude of William of Orange and the "serene magnanimity" of Marlborough, never fail to impress; but there is also a charm in following the experience of an officer who served under them in a marching regiment or in subordinate command, for in so doing we seem to pursue a hitherto undiscovered by-way parallel to the great high road, which leads by nooks before unnoticed, and lends new interest to a familiar journey.

It would be difficult to overrate the advantage which the study of history has reaped in recent years from the opening up of immense stores of private correspondence and authentic documents long preserved in silence in the charter-chests and muniment rooms of old country houses. The materials have been in many cases afforded which enabled us to "contrast the hidden motive with the avowed pretext of public transactions," and if the revelation of the record, which was not written for history, sometimes "gilds refined gold," it sometimes explodes reputations. But there are scattered deposits as well as rich veins of such literary treasures, and there sometimes lurk in private repositories a few papers, which have a value of their own, either as contributing to the elucidation of obscure events, or as affording illustrations of types of individuals or classes who were important factors in national life. Having occasion sometime ago to look through the contents of such a cabinet, we came upon a series of commissions and a few other documents, the dates of which corresponded in so interesting a manner with those of great public events, that the desire seized us, if possible, to reconstruct the career of the individual to whom they related. The period was an enticing one, for it was that of the generation who witnessed the final establishment of the Protestant character of this country, and the satisfactory settlement on a firm basis of the British Constitution.

The materials were somewhat scanty, for the home, to which the son of the soldier whose name heads these pages removed, was "harried" by Gordon of Glenbucket's Highlanders in the Forty-five, and such of his papers as had found a resting-place elsewhere did not escape perils of fire. He was the third son of William Ferguson of Badifurrow—a mansion situated on the braes that slope down to the Don, not [very] far from that prominent feature of Aberdeenshire landscape, Benachie,—who represented Inverurie in the first Scottish Parliament after the Restoration, which from the personal energy displayed by its members in celebrating the fact that "the King enjoyed his own again," obtained the designation of "the Drunken Parliament." Tradition carried back the connection of his progenitors with the locality to the 14th century, and it has been said—with what truth is impossible now to ascertain—that one of the name "afforded ready and manly aid" to King Robert Bruce in the battle fought there, which initiated the chain of victories that culminated at Bannockburn. The Laird of Badifurrow left his property to his second son, for the eldest imbibed opinions unpalatable to his cavalier sentiments, and betaking himself to England, kept up little communication with his relatives in the North. History has assigned to him emphatically the title of "the Plotter." His varied experience embraced both parties and three competing ecclesiastical systems; he was for long the right hand man, and nominally the chaplain, of Lord Shaftesbury, who perhaps more than any other statesman is entitled to be called the founder of the Whig party. When "the false Achitophel" fled into exile, the "Judas" of Dryden's satire was one of the two friends who alone remained with him to the last, and Shaftesbury "died in Ferguson's arms in Holland." He has been described as "the evil genius of the unfortunate Monmouth," and as he turned Jacobite and High Churchman after the Revolution, he secured the personal dislike of Burnet and the polemical denunciation of Macaulay. But the perusal of some of his own letters leads to a more charitable construction of his career than annalists have yet recorded; and a record he has left of the most involved passage in his life fits in remarkably with facts previously ascertained, and casts a fresh light on a fascinating and melancholy drama in English History. Though no careers could be more dissimilar, yet on one or two occasions the paths in life of "Ferguson the Plotter" and his soldier brother curiously crossed.*

* "v. Robert Ferguson the Plotter." D. Douglas, Edinburgh, 1887.

The third son of a numerous family, the subject of our sketch, went like many other young Scotsmen of the time to find a career or a *quietus* in "the Lawlands o' Holland." For a small and impecunious country like Scotland, abounding with turbulent spirits, the old "Scots Brigade" was an admirable institution. It had for long been the fortune of the northern kingdom to provide other countries with their best soldiers; the fame of the Scots Guards in France was attested by many a stricken field, from the time when

> "Swinton set the lance in rest
> That tamed of yore the sparkling crest
> Of Clarence's Plantagenet!"

and Gustavus Adolphus, "the Lion of the North," owed many of his victories to the valour of his Scottish regiments. The Reformation in Scotland, and the revolt of the United Provinces opened a new field for the military spirit of the race, and so early as the year 1572, the famous brigade was formed, which won for itself the designation of "the Bulwark of the Republic." In 1578 the Scots regiments in the Dutch service bore the brunt of the action in the battle of Reminaut against the Spaniards, "fighting without armour and in their shirts," and when more than 200 years later, owing to the spread of revolutionary principles in Holland, the traditions of "the old Brigade" were carried on in the 94th regiment of the British army—it was among the oldest regular troops in Europe, and could boast of a long record of battles, storms, and triumphs won in "the classic land of fortified defence." *

At the time of which we write, these troops combined the service of the States with allegiance to their own Sovereign, and as "the three Dutch regiments" formed a part of the fighting strength of Britain, while under the name of "the Scots Brigade," they constituted the most effective portion of the forces of Holland. Graham of Claverhouse was serving under their colours when he saved the life of William of Orange at Seneff, and it had been the failure to give him the promised command of one of the Scots regiments, which caused him to declare that "he would not serve

---

* Appendix, 1. "The position of the Scots Brigade," and commissions there printed.

a Prince who had broken his word." He was destined to meet in the pass of Killiecrankie the very officer in whose favour he had been overlooked.

Young Ferguson, joining the Scots Brigade, entered the best school of discipline and practical warfare which the circumstances of the age afforded. The brigade, which had deteriorated owing to the admixture of foreign elements, had recently been reorganised by General Mackay, acting upon his spirited reply to the Prince of Orange, whom he assured that if it was recruited in Scotland, and commissions given to Scotsmen of good family, it would soon be as good as ever; and in 1685 it received a warm tribute of admiration from King James, who little realized for what that powerful weapon was next to be unsheathed. It is probable that, as was common at the time, his military service began as a gentleman-volunteer. His first commission, dated 12th June, 1677, was as Quarter Master in Colonel Macdonell's regiment. On 9th September of the following year, he received one as "Vendrigh" in Captain van Zuylen's company, and on 21st February, 1682, another as Lieutenant in Captain Cuningham's company. On 10th June, 1685, a similar document describes him as Lieutenant of Captain Middleton's company," by exchange." That very day, in London, Luttrell made the note in his diary:—" The three Scotch regiments that are in the service of the Dutch, are sent for over, in order to be sent into Scotland against the rebells." But the insurrection, headed by the Earl of Argyle in the West of Scotland, was quelled before their services were required, and they were directed to London, threatened from another quarter. The unfortunate Monmouth, "so beautiful, so brave," had been received with enthusiasm by the peasantry of the West of England, and King James was mustering all his forces to crush him. On the third of July, "the three Scotch regiments which came from Holland, were drawn up in Blackheath before his Majestie, and the next day early they marched towards the west." They were, however, too late for the fight on Sedgemoor, in which Lieutenant Ferguson's more notorious brother, on the other side, had slightly forgotten his clerical character, and immediately returned to Holland.

Three years pass and another commission is followed by another voyage to England. But a great deal had happened in these three years, and the expedition of 1688 was under other banners and different auspices. Never perhaps had the tide of loyalty in England been in higher flood than when James succeeded to the throne, for the memory of the Ryehouse Plot was emphasized by the impending rebellion of Monmouth; and among the many loyal addresses which greeted the King's accession had been one from "the officers of the Scots and English regiments in Holland." It was the distinction of the policy he pursued to have changed all that; he had alienated the very classes who had most faithfully supported and suffered most for his father; and assailing the national church, he had converted the fidelity of a triumphant party into smouldering hostility, and prepared that coalition of parties, under the watchword of "Liberty, Property, and Religion," which made the Revolution of 1688 an enduring national act, and not the temporary *coup d'état* of a faction. It was a significant fact that when, in 1687, he recalled the British troops in Holland, and the States, while forbidding the men to leave the colours, left the officers at liberty to follow their own inclinations, only 60 out of 240 obeyed the call. On the 22nd of March, 1688, Ferguson obtained his company, being appointed to Captain George Hamilton's, which had become vacant. But the importance of the rise in rank, and, it so happened, of the impending occasion, was typfied by a larger document, dated 1st April, 1688. While his previous commissions, including that of 22nd March, are signed simply by "G. Prince d'Orange," this one is in duplicate, flowing both from the Prince of Orange and "De Stated Generael der Vereeniehde Nederlanden," and is engrossed on two pretentious pieces of parchment.

Captain Ferguson found himself on this occasion for a short time on the same side as his brother Robert, for both were on board the fleet which carried the Prince of Orange to the throne of Britain. When William disembarked in Torbay the first troops to land were Mackay's veterans of "the Old Brigade." They marched with him to London, but did not long remain there, for on 13th March, 1689, "the three Scotch regiments that came with the king from Holland went down the river in the companies' barges, to go on board some ships to carry them to Leith in Scotland, to secure the peace of that kingdom." On the 25th

of the same month, the Scottish Convention of Estates granted
"warrant to the magistrates of Edinburgh to quarter two regiments
under the command of Major-General Mackay, in Leith and the
suburbs of Edinburgh." For by that time it was "up with the
bonnets of bonny Dundee," and the authorities were not sorry
to see the "wild westland Whigs" who thronged the Grassmarket,
and the levies which Leven gathered off the streets of Edinburgh,
supported by regular troops, and were eager to "acknowledge the
great kindness and care of the King of England" in sending them.
The next fact in Ferguson's career, as to which his own papers
speak, presents him as having attained Field-officer's rank,
and entrusted with duty of difficulty and responsibility. But
before that time arrived he had probably seen hard fighting.
His regiment, which was that called, from its commander,
Brigadier Balfour's, till Balfour fell before the Highland claymore
at Killiecrankie, and afterwards Colonel Lauder's regiment, was
one of those under Mackay's command during the campaign
marked by that celebrated battle, in which "the vanquished
triumphed and the victors mourned." Lauder, then Lieutenant-
Colonel of the regiment he was so soon to command, was
in charge of the advanced guard—"picked men of the Dutch
brigade"—which Mackay pushed forward to secure the Pass of
Killiecrankie, when he set out from Perth for Blair; and when
the Lowland army debouched upon the open ground at the head
of the gorge, it was Lauder's Fusiliers who first felt the enemy.
According to Mackay's own account of his defeat:—"Lieutenant-
Colonel Lauder was advantageously posted upon the left of all
on a little hill wreathed with trees, with his party of two hundred
of the choice of our army; but did as little as the rest of that
hand, whether by his or his men's fault is not well known,
for the General would never make search into the failings of
that business, because they were a little too generally committed."
In another account he says that Lauder was "abandoned by his
party, and laboured without success to rally them"; and from the
reflection of another contemporary, that "it is a pity to give green
men to good men to command them," it would seem that the
officers did their duty, but were not supported by the rank and
file. Luttrel mentions that letters from Scotland reported "that

the fight was maintained very sharply for some time, but two of the Scots regiments that came from Holland would not fight, which occasioned a disorder among our men." Was it the recollection of old times, and a reminiscence of the Cavalier who "wore a white plumach" on the field of Seneff, which unnerved the picked men of the Dutch brigade? The Stuart papers mention a Captain Ferguson as having been taken prisoner at Killiecrankie; and Captain Crichton, the old dragoon and "persecutor" of the western Covenanters, whose recollections Dean Swift took down when living in the North of Ireland many years after, mentions that "next day, though victorious, the Highlanders suffered their prisoners to depart on parole that they would never take up arms against King James—Colonel Ferguson only excepted on account of his more than ordinary zeal for the new establishment." The incident affords one of those curious coincidences and contrasts which give so much of the life and colour to the dry bones of history. For one of the first acts of the Royalists after the Restoration had been to collect the scattered remains of the Marquis of Montrose from every "port" and "airt" to which they had been dispersed, and to celebrate the "True Funerals" of the "Great Cavalier," and the companion of his campaigns who had suffered along with him, Sir William Hay of Delgaty, in the Church of St. Giles. Among those who took part in the ceremony was Captain Ferguson's father, the Laird of Badifurrow, who bore "the gumphion" before the bier of the Knight of Delgaty. It would be strange indeed if to the ears of the son, a prisoner of war, had floated the strains of "the Burial March of Dundee." The character given him by Crichton quite accords with what tradition has preserved as to his sentiments, and this little incident very well illustrates the contrast between "the Usurpation" and the Revolution of 1688, which indeed carried out the constitutional policy of wise reform originally advocated by Hyde and Falkland in England, and by Montrose in Scotland. An allusion in a letter of his own many years later indicates that Captain Ferguson saw no break of continuity between his father's loyalty to King Charles and his own fidelity to King William. If he was taken among the few who were left standing at their posts, when the mass of the Lowland army broke away before the sweeping onset of the

clansmen, he must have been exchanged * or escaped,† for within
a year he was conducting important enterprises as Major without
any reflection on his reputation, and much relied on by his
commanding-officer.

It had for some time been a favourite project with Mackay
to fix a thorn in the side of the Highlanders who adhered to King
James, by constructing a fort and depôt on the West Coast in an
advantageous position, for controlling the mainland districts of
Lochaber and Morven, bridling the island of Mull, where the
Jacobites were very strong, and to which they sent their prisoners,
and cutting communication between King James' supporters in
Scotland, and the army of Irish and French auxiliaries he was
himself at the head of in Ireland. Owing to the difficulties
with which "poor, honest General-Major Mackay"—as Dalrymple
calls him—had to deal, arising from the ambitions and intrigues
which were rife in the Council at Edinburgh, and the lack of
energy displayed in seconding his scheme on the part of the
political authorities, a considerable time elapsed before he could
get his project carried out. "At last," however, "he obtained his
desire with regard to the fort at Inverlochy." The king ordered
three 30 gun frigates with arms, ammunition, and implements to
the West Coast of Scotland, and as the season was far advanced,
Mackay proposed to the Council, "that in the first place, in order
"the more to intimidate the Highlanders, and force many of them
"to keep at home to guard their own property, a detachment of
"600 chosen men should, in the meantime, be sent in the ships
"which were to sail with the materials and other necessaries."
But "because of the emptiness of their coffers they were not
"able to despatch the detachment; and if the General had not got
"the Provost and city of Glasgow to furnish the ships and materials,

* On 3rd September, 1689, the Privy Council wrote to General Mackay
authorising an exchange of prisoners, "with such as you think meetest out of
the enemies' hands." No Colonel Ferguson is recorded as present at Killiecrankie, and Crichton apparently gives the rank by which he was better known
for many years, to the Captain of the Stuart papers.

† The Clan Ferguson of Athole joined Dundee's army a day or two after
Killiecrankie; it has been said that there was some old tradition of far-away
kinship between them and their Aberdeenshire namesakes, and possibly in this
may lie the secret of the Captain's good fortune.

"it had not been done for a month after, whereby the whole de-
"signed advantage of sending the detachment had been lost."
It was in the beginning of March, 1690, he writes, that "he
"engaged the city of Glasgow to hire ships, and make the neces-
"sary provisions for the speedy despatch of the 600 men, which
"he designed for the enemy's coast to make diversion under the
"command of Major Ferguson, a resolute well-affected officer
"to whose discretion and diligence he trusted much. He en-
"gaged the Magistrates of the said city also to furnish and
"send away with the detachment 5000 palisades, with 500 spades,
"shovels, and pickaxes, to make up 2000 in all with the 1500
"sent down from England, which he had ordered to Glasgow to
"be sent away with the party." The historian of the House and
Clan of Mackay, after quoting this passage, adds in a note a
characteristic anecdote of the officer who had been thus selected
as suited "to make diversion." "When in Flanders he had on
"one occasion volunteered to go with a small party to guard a great
"number of prisoners to a considerable distance, after others had
"signified a wish to decline the service as being too hazardous.
"For the greater safety he cut the latchets of the prisoners' small-
"clothes, which obliged them to march with one hand behind to
"hold them up. He had a brother of a very different cast known
"by the name of Robert the Plotter." That worthy indeed had
now become as hot a partisan of the exiled house as he had
previously been of Monmouth and William of Orange, and was
deeply engaged with Sir James Montgomery, the Earl of
Annandale, Lord Ross, and others in a plot to combine the
extreme Presbyterians and Jacobites in an effort for the restoration of James. An incident which General Mackay thus notices
in his "Memoirs" proves that he had hoped to persuade his
brother to join in this intrigue, which, occurring at a very critical
moment, and coinciding with renewed efforts in the Highlands,
great exertions on the part of the French, and those endeavours
in Ireland which were only defeated by the battle of the Boyne,
caused much anxiety to Queen Mary and her advisers. "About
the middle of April," says Mackay, "though he (the General),
to avoid all suspicion of himself, had delivered to the Commissary
Melville's creature £4000 which the King had sent to the

General towards the expedition: yet Major Ferguson was kept up about five weeks waiting for his provisions; and not only so, but the club who had joined in Parliament with the Jacobites, thinking to overrule that which was called the Court party, essayed to debauch Major Ferguson, after it had been publicly known that the General had appointed him to command the detachment of land forces along with the frigates: to whom the said Major, who is a vigorous and well-affected man, discovered all their proposals not silencing a letter from a very near relation of his own to the same purpose; whereof the General gave present notice to the Commissioner, and afterwards to the King." In writing to King William,* Mackay described Major Ferguson as "*personne de probité et d'honneur comme aussi fidèle et affectionné au service de votre Majesté.*"

In the beginning of May the preparations, thanks to the city of Glasgow, were complete, and from a burgess ticket of that town, dated 7th May, 1690, in favour of "James Ferguson, Major of the regiment of Colonel Lauder," it appears that the Magistrates of the Metropolis of the West combined their services to the cause with a personal compliment to the commander. On the 15th of May he set sail from Greenock. The instructions "for Major Ferguson, appointed to command in chief the detachment of 600 men, which are to be shipped at Greenock, and to go about to the isles and the coast of Lochaber, and for Captain Pottinger commanding their Majesties' ship the *Dartmouth*, with the rest of the squade under his command,"† were of considerable length and couched in quaint phraseology. The importance of harmony between the two services and commanders was insisted on. Nothing active was to be done but "upon visible and apparent advantages and humane assurance of success." A descent on Mull, with the assistance of the Campbells, was, however, suggested; and Ferguson was ordered to open communications and co-operate with the Laird of MacLeod. They were to "use with all the rigour of military executions such as shall continue obstinate in their rebellion with this proviso that women and children be not touched or wronged in their persons." And one touch shows distinctly the

---

* Lettre écrite au Roy le 16 Avril 1690 d' Edimbourg.
† Printed in the Appendix to " Mackay's Memoirs."

hand of the worthy old officer whom Burnet describes as the most pious of soldiers. "The said Major commanding in-chief shall have speciall care his men be keeped under exact discipline, both as soldiours and christians, to hinder cursing and swearing and all other unchristian and disorderly customs, and to chastise in their purs and persons such as persist in them after intimation."

The conduct of the expedition fully justified Mackay's choice of a commander, and expectations of the advantages to be gained. "The gross of the rebels," he says, "particularly such as dwelt near the sea, with the inhabitants of the isles, staid at home to guard their country against the frigates with Ferguson's detachment, at the very noise whereof they were very much terrified." It prevented the Western Clans "from coming in any considerable numbers to the assistance of Buchan and Cannon." Another writer observes that, as a consequence of its appearance, the "small islands between Kintire and Mull had put themselves under the protection of the Government, and the Earl of Seaforth with some others of the principal Highlanders were inclinable to do the same." On the 30th May the Privy Council, being informed "that Major Ferguson is arrived at the island of Mull, and is now lying at Dunstaffnage, and that several of the rebels have got together in a body within that isle in and about the castle of Dowart," ordained the Earl of Argyle to order Colin Campbell of Ardkinglass to levy 600 men and march to reinforce him. The Council allowed the Earl to nominate his own officers, and recommended the Lords Commisioners of the Treasury to order 400 bolls of meal to be sent to Inverary for the use of the 600 men. A letter of the time,* addressed "for Angus Campbell, of Kilberry," shows the steps taken to put this force in the field, the motives that were appealed to, and the blended influence of feudal power, and clan attachment wielded by the House of Argyle.

"Edinburgh, 4th June, 1690.

"Loveing Cousein,

"Their Majesties' Privy Councill hes (ordered) us to raise six hundred men to goe to Dunstaffnage to (meet) Major Ferguson

---

* Preserved among the Kilberry papers, and printed in the Appendix to the "Memoirs of Lochiel."

there. That this may be the better effectuate, wee ordered Sir Colin Campbell of Ardkinlass to go from this to (meet) you at Inverary, upon Thursday, the 12th day of this instant, for appointing these men to be raised, and for other (things pertaining to) the good of the country. Wee entreat you faill (not to come) there at that time and give your advyse, assistance, and (concurrance) in this matter. Wee expect that all of you will readily (comply) with the desyre of the Councill, both for the country's (good and) ours. And we hope, by your concurrance in this, (to have the) shyre exeemed from their resting public burdens. Those (who) will not concurr, they may expect little favour of this nature, (and a dale of) trouble for their disobedience, that at present they may (avoid). There is four hundred bolls of victuall ordered to be sent . . . for maintaining those six hundred men, and what else (they will) need, Major Ferguson will see them provided in. (What) farther we have to say in this matter, and what directions (are necessary) thereanent, shall be sent by Ardkinlass.

" We are,
" Your loveing Cousin,
" ARGYLL.

" I own I have ever found you most readie in what concerned me. I desyre you, upon this occasion, (to be) very active, and I have ordered you the command of the partie."

An armistice, which had been the result of some make-believe negotiations, was soon recalled, and Mackay having sent an order to Ferguson to meet him at Inverlochy, set out from Perth on the 18th of June with about 3000 horse and foot. On the 6th of July, Lord Melville wrote to the King :—"I had not account from Major-General Mackay till just now, a post has come in from Inverlochy, showing that Major Ferguson, after he had burnt some of the islands, and taken assurance of some others not to join the rebels, not being strong enough to land in the Island of Mull, had come to Inverlochy, the place where Mackay designs to make the fort, and encamped at Lochyeall House this day sennight, and stayed till Mackay came to him, which he did Thursday or Frayday last." For a Government detachment to encamp at Lochiel House, was certainly establishing itself comfortably in the lion's den ; and an account of the previous proceedings of the expedition is furnished in a despatch from Captain Pottinger to Lord Melville dated, "Aboard the *Dartmouth* in Duart Road, 19th July, 1690." Captain Pottinger excuses himself for not having written since leaving Greenock, on the ground of having been since then "scarce 48 hours in one place without motion," and of having "referred to Major Ferguson, who assured me of the tender of my most humble duty to your Grace upon several occasions, and that he would be more particular therein than I could or would have expected from the land part on't. But since Major Ferguson (who is a man of great diligence, zealously affected to the present Government, and brave enough) is parted," Captain Pottinger had to write his own despatches, and thus related what had been done. "We divided our squades and boats they burning and destroying one way, our ships with the Major left nothing undone that was to be done the other way, in burning houses, breaking boats, and destroying the substance of such as was in actual rebellion; nor hath our appearance upon the coast had less effect in keeping these McClains of Mull, McDonalds, &c., all at whom (if possible) to preserve their interest; so that joining was prevented." The *Dartmouth*, on board which this despatch was written, was one of the three ships that had relieved Derry not long before, having covered the advance of the *Mountjoy* when she broke the boom that stretched across the Foyle. * Mackay had arrived at Inverlochy on the 3rd July, and

* Captain Pottinger, who wrote the despatch, was a gallant officer, but the *Dartmouth* was destined to be his last command. A record of his services is found in a resolution of the Scots Privy Council, dated 1st January, 1691, upon a petition presented by Thomas Pottinger, "the Sovereign of Belfast," on behalf of the widow and children of his deceased brother, Captain Edward Pottinger, commander of the frigate called the *Dartmouth*. The Privy Council recommended the widow and children to "the King's Sovereign Majesty his favour and bounty," on account of Captain Pottinger's "great zeal, and the signal services performed by him." The record bears that he had "evidenced great zeal and affection for the Protestant interest, as is not unknown to all that ever knew him." He had levied a company of men at his own expense, and defended Coleraine against the Irish army—the enemy being beat off "by his courage and skill in levelling and discharging the guns," all which was testified by a formal document, vouched by the Mayor and Aldermen of Coleraine. As commander of a yacht, he had served with daring and credit at the siege of Carrickfergus, which was similarly testified by General Douglas. As Captain of the *Dartmouth*, which "was ordered to cruise in the West Seas for their

the construction of the fort, which Ferguson had commenced, was rapidly proceeded with. It was called Fort-William, after the King, and formed the first of the chain of fortresses, which raised at the centre and both ends of the great glen of Albyn, for years were so powerful a check on the unruly spirit of the Highlands. "I recommend," wrote Mackay to Lord Melville, "earnestly to your Grace the care of this post, which I look upon as the most important of the kingdom at present, and that which will at length make such as would sell their credit and service at such a deare rait to the King of no greater use nor no more necessary to him than a Lothian or Fyf Laird; therefore, by no means let it be neglected though other things should be postponed."

Before Mackay left Fort-William, on the 15th of July, he ordered a detachment to the Island of Mull. This detachment, though countermanded on the news of the naval reverse off Beachy Head, was subsequently despatched, and was commanded by Ferguson, for the Stuart papers record that the Highlanders who had received officers, ammunition, and provisions from James in Ireland, and had taken arms to second Sir James Montgomery's intrigues in Parliament, were "repulsed rather than defeated by Sir Thomas Livingston in the county of Moray, and by Major Ferguson in the Island of Mull." If his success was equal to that of Livingston on "the Haughs of Cromdale," thus similarly described, the repulse of the Jacobites must have been a total rout. "Major Ferguson," says Oldmixon, "was very successful against the rebels in the Island of Mull, while his brother, that vile apostate from all principles of morality, religion, and liberty, was in the depths of the Assassination and Invasion Plots in England." And again :—"The progress of Major Ferguson in the Isle of

---

Majesties service in this kingdom, it is well known to the said Lords of Council with what faithfulness and diligence he behaved himself in the said service, and with what assiduity and carefulness he exonered himselfe of the trust and commission given unto him therein at all occasions, from the latter end of May that he came here till the month of October last, when by the violence of a great tempest and storme as happened not in many years at the dispensation and pleasure of God, he, with his men, ship, and furniture did all perish, (four or fyve excepted) to the exceeding grief and loss of his relict and fatherless children."

Mull was so prosperous that it obliged Sir John MacLean, the proprietor, to submit to their Majesties' Government and deliver up his castles to their forces." That his discharge of the duty entrusted to him received the approval of his commanding officer is proved by the General recommending him for promotion in a letter directly addressed to the King himself.* "*Et comme le bien du service,*" wrote Mackay, "*m' oblige de luy representer ceux qui en sont capables et si attachent avec zelle, le Lieutenant-Colonel Buchan merit que votre Majesté luy donne une meilleure poste, et Ferguson seroit bien plus capable de commander le regiment de Lauder que Balfour,† s'il y avoit moyen d'accomoder celluy-ci autrement.*" It affords an instructive illustration of the division of opinion which prevailed in Scotland at the time, to observe that of the two officers here recommended as zealous adherents of the Protestant succession, one was the brother of the Commander-in-Chief of the opposing army, while the brother of the other had been arrested a few months before by the order of King William, who was desirous that information should be forwarded on the strength of which he might be sent to Scotland, as otherwise it would be necessary by the law of England to release him. Ten years were to elapse before the measure that has been called the Scottish *Habeas Corpus* Act took its place in the statute book. Both soldiers, too, were Aberdeenshire men, for the Buchans were brothers of the Laird of Auchmacoy.

It would seem that after the reduction of the Western Islands, Ferguson's capacity and zeal were utilised on the Lowland side of the Highland line, for the records of the Scots Privy Council show that on 26th May, 1691, Sir Thomas Livingstone, Mackay's successor as Commander-in-Chief, laid before them a letter "directed to him by Major Ferguson in Perth, dated the 25th day of May instant, bearing that the prisoner which Major Munro was sending from Castle Blair made his escape about a mile from Perth, and that the ensign with the most of the party are gone after him, and that he has sent forward the money to Sir Thomas, and giving account that Sir Thomas's orders which the Major

---

* Lettre écrite au Roy peu de temps après le construction de Fort-William.
† There had been two Balfours in the regiment at Killiecrankie. One was killed and one was taken prisoner.

caused publish at the church doors, had so good effect that Kindrogin, who commanded a party of the (thieves?) was killed the last week with two or three of his followers in Glen Prossen, and since they have sent several more of that gang prisoners to Perth, and that the whole country do solicit they may be hanged, or an order got for their tryall or transportation." The Council promptly ordained a Commission of Justiciary to be drawn, directed to the Magistrates of Perth, "for trying and judging such of the Highland thieves or robbers as are presently in the tolbooth of Perth."

The commencement of the Inverlochy Expedition had seen Ferguson admitted a Burgess of Glasgow, and its successful termination, and his subsequent services were recognized in a similar manner by a grant of the freedom of the City of Edinburgh on 30th October, 1691.

Within six months he was again in the Low countries, for his next commission as Lieutenant-Colonel in Monro's Regiment, which, unlike the others, is in the English form and superscribed by King William, is dated "at Our Camp at Lembeck the first day of August, 1692," just a few days after the bloody field of Steinkirk, where the British division, outnumbered and unsupported, had for long sustained unequal combat, and at last, exhausted and overwhelmed, only sullenly yielded to the impetuous charge of the famous Household Brigade,

"The dread of Europe, and the pride of France."

"Let us see how these English bull-dogs will fight," had been the response of Count Solms to requests for reinforcement, and brave old Mackay, ordered to a post he knew to be untenable, after pointing out the fact in vain, had gone forward for the last time with the words "The will of the Lord be done." His division left 3000 dead on the field, and, amongst others, Lauder's Regiment was severely handled, its Colonel being taken prisoner.

II.

COLONEL OF THE CAMERONIANS.

"HAD Count Solmes, Trim, done the same at the battle of Steinkirk, said Yorick, drolling a little upon the corporal, who had been run over by a dragoon in the retreat—he had saved thee—Saved! said Trim, interrupting Yorick, and finishing the sentence for him after his own fashion, he had saved five battalions, an', please your reverence, every soul of them. There was Cutt's, —continued the corporal, clapping the fore-finger of his right hand upon the thumb of the left, and counting round his hand,—there was Cutt's—Mackay's —Angus's—Graham's—and Leven's, all cut to pieces: and so had the English Life-guards, too, had it not been for some regiments upon the right, who marched up boldly to their relief, and received the enemy's fire in the face before any one of their own platoons discharged a musket. . . . . Had we drubbed them soundly at Steinkirk, they would not have fought us at Landen."—*Tristram Shandy.*

AT Steinkirk, Ferguson had served for the last time in the old Scots Brigade, for the regiment to which he was now appointed was the famous one that had been raised three years before among the followers of Richard Cameron, the sternest of the Covenanters of the West. Its first Colonel, the youthful Earl of Angus,* had fallen in the recent battle, and Lieutenant-Colonel Monro succeeding to the command, Ferguson was appointed in his place. Short as had hitherto been the career of the Cameronian Regiment, it had previously lost its Lieutenant-Colonel when Cleland was killed at Dunkeld, and a year after he entered it Ferguson obtained the Colonelcy, when Monro died of sore sickness after the battle of Landen (or Neerwinden). Unique in its origin and organisation, it had, when embodied, 1200 strong on the holm of Douglas on 14th May, 1689, been formed on the model of a Presbytery,

---

* It was known first as Angus's, then as Munro's, then as Ferguson's, later as Stair's and Preston's, for long as the 26th (Cameronians), and now as the First Battalion of "The Cameronians Scottish Rifles."

with a minister to the regiment and an elder to each company. Indeed, "their minister" exercised an influence not always conducive to good discipline and military subordination, and on one occasion his dislike to being quartered at Fort-William had been the source of some anxiety to the governor of that garrison. Mackay had at that time observed—" Angus's regiment ought to have a man of service put upon their head," and even in the Low Countries their chaplain continued to be a marked figure. In a diary of a tour in Holland in the year 1696, made by a west country Laird, William Mure of Glanderstone (afterwords of Caldwell), he records that at Gemblois, on 27th June—" I went to Colonel Ferguson's regiment near to the rear of the lines, and heard worthy Mr. Shields preach." And long after the Cameronians had little in common with the fierce zealots, who so gallantly defended Dunkeld against the Highlanders, it is said the tradition was maintained which placed a Bible in the knapsack of every soldier.

On 25th August 1693, shortly after the hard fought battle of Landen, Colonel Ferguson succeeded to the command of the Cameronians.* He held it for twelve years, during most of which they served in the Low Countries in the campaigns of William, and subsequently under the brighter auspices of Marlborough. Indeed, when the British army was reduced after the Peace of Ryswick in 1697, owing to a vote of the House of Commons that "all the forces raised since the year 1680 should be disbanded," they were for some time retained in Holland, in Dutch pay. A Commission to Colonel Ferguson, as Captain in his own regiment, dated 1st January, 1698, is in Dutch, and in the same form as those of the "Schotsche Brigade," except that it flows in the name of "*Sijne Majesteijt*," and is signed "William R." † On the 20th

---

* The Calendar of the Treasury papers contains this entry—"December 4 and 7, 1694, Paymaster Fox, his memorial for a warrant to pay £1800 to the Commissioners of Transports to be by them paid to Colonel Ferguson, for transport and provision of recruits shipped from Scotland to the Low Countries, dated 4th December, 1694.

Letter signed, W. Lowndes, on the same subject, dated 7th December, 1694."

† I am indebted to the courtesy of the officials of the "Rijks Archief" at

of the following February * leave was granted by "*Walrad by der Gratien Godes, Furst van Nassau, Grave tot Sarbrucken, en Sarwerden, Heere tot Lahr Wiesbaden en Idsteyn, &c. Velt Maerschalck Generael van sijne Keyserlijcke Majesteyt, als mede van den Staet der Vereenighde Nederlanden, ende Gouverneur van's Hertogenbosch, &c.," to "den Hre. Ferguson, Colonel oover een Regiment Schotten te voet in dienste van Lande . . sich van den dienst te mogen absenteren, en naer Schotlandt te gaen tot ver-sightinge van syne affaires.*" One of the affairs which required his personal attention, was probably of a matrimonial character, for he was married about this time to Helen, daughter of James Drummond of Cultmalindie.† The marriage was, unfortunately, of short duration, for Mrs. Ferguson soon died, leaving two little

the Hague, for the following extracts, which clearly authenticate an interesting page in the history of the Cameronian regiment.

"Resolutie Staten Generaal 29th October, 1697. Zijne Hoogheid de Prins van Oranjé geest kennis voornemens te zijn met het volgend jaar de Schotsche regimenten die sedert den jare 1689, in Zr Ms bezoldiging zijn geweest in dienst van den Staat terug te geven."

"Resolutie Raad van State, 12th December, 1697. Teruggekeerd 6 Schotsche regimenten be-paling van de wijze waarop zij ter repartitie van de verschillende provincien zullen worden gebracht.

Gelderland.	Lauder.
Holland.	Colyear.
	Ferguson.
	Schratnaver.
	Murray.
Zeeland.	Hamilton."

* Printed form filled up in writing.

†The Drummonds of Cultmalindie, an estate near the City of Perth, were descended through the houses of Invermay and Drummonderinoch, from Malcolm Drummond of Cargill, 11th chief of the name, and progenitor of the Dukes of Perth. Their family history thus comprised the dark tragedy of Celtic savagery which furnished Sir Walter Scott with the character of Allan Macaulay in the *Legend of Montrose*. Who, that has read either the novel, or the *Tales of a Grandfather*, can forget the scene in the hall of Ardvoirlich when the lady of the house, offering her hospitality to the murderers of her brother, fled from the sight of his head upon the table, or the other in the old church of Balquhidder, recorded even more graphically in the quaint words of the Privy Council proclamation which ranged "the ire of the Drummonds" on the side of the Law when engaged in "taking sweet revenge for the death of their cousin, Drummond-Ernoch?" v. App. iv.

infants, a son and a daughter. The one trait of her character that has descended is recorded in the quaint words of an old memoir which describes her as "a seeker and server of God." A few years before Colonel Ferguson had acquired the estates of Balmakellie and Kirktonhill* on the Kincardineshire bank of the North Esk, and it must have been a very welcome order which soon afterwards recalled the Cameronians to Scotland and stationed them at Perth. His leave (originally for three months) must have been extended, for, on 9th November, 1698, the freedom of Montrose was presented to "Collonell James Fergusone of Balmakellie." It is probable that the regiment came over in April, 1699, for in August of the previous year, he describes himself in granting a bond as "Commander of one of the Scots foot regiments in the service of the States Generall of the United Provinces," while a document attested as "compared with the books in the Exchequer," and headed "Abstract of the money due to Colonel Ferguson's regiment on the Establishment, from the 14th April, 1699, to the 1st December, 1700," may be taken as fixing the date of the transfer from Holland to Great Britain.† This paper gives a

---

* These Kincardineshire estates were sold by his son, who purchased, instead, the lands of Kinmundy and Coynach in Buchan.

† The document among the Kinmundy papers agrees exactly with the entries in the Dutch records.

"Resolutie van de Staten Generaal, 6 September, 1698. Ontvangen eene missive van Zijne Majesteit waarbij wordt voorgesteld te licentieeren en naar Schotlandt terug te zenden het regimenten van den Kolonel Hamilton benevens de twee jongste compagnien van ieder de 5 overige regimenten, in het geheel 22 compagnien te voet, waartoe Zijne Majesteit wordt geauthoriseerd,"

"Resolutie van den Raad van State van 15 April, 1699. Is gelesen een request van James Ferguson en Johan Lord Strathnaver, Kolonels van twee Schotsche regimenten, te kennen gevende in substancie dat zij patent bekomen hebbende om te verlaten den dienst van den Lande en weder te keeren naar Schotland, te Rotterdam gekomen zijnde om de reis van daar voort te zetten, &c. Verzoek om Restitutie van eenige gelden."

At the date of the Scotch document the arrears due to the officers of Colonel Ferguson's regiment were £2443 7s., with an additional sum of £1632 15s. 6d. for cloathing and reckonings. The Colonel was £273 in arrear, the Lieutenant-Colonel £204 15s, the Major £177 9s., each of the Captains £109 4s., most of the Lieutenants £54 12s., and most of the Ensigns £40 19s. each. The whole

glimpse of the *personnel* of the officers, and shows both a touch of the clannish sentiment of the Scots nation, and how thoroughly the regiment was officered by Scotsmen. Commissions as Captains were held cumulatively by the Colonel, Lieut-Colonel, and Major, and the other Captains were—Alex. Campbell, James Cranston, Henry Stewart, John Blackader (afterwards Governor of Stirling, and author of a diary, which has been published in his memoir by Dr. Crichton), George Murray, Andrew Monro, and James Aikman. Among the subalterns were several of the Colonel's own name. A Lieutenant John Ferguson was Adjutant, while there were three ensigns, John, Robert, and James Ferguson. The last was possibly his son, who certainly a few years later formed an instance of the practice commemorated in the story of "the Major crying for his parritch;" and two nephews, called respectively John and Robert, had entered the army. William Hamilton is designated as Captain-Lieutenant, and the names of the other Subalterns are the Scotch ones of Wilson (two), Lawson, Lindsay, Dickson, Gordon, Fairbairn, Boyd, Murray, Haddo, Maitland (two), Douglas, Bernard, Gray, Seton, Drummond, Glendinning.

amount payable to the regiment for the time mentioned was £10,593 16s. sterling. This was made up thus :—" For full pay for 8 companys for last 14 days in April, 1699, £221 4s. To Do. for 2 companys for the last week of April, 1699, £25 4s. To Do. for 10 companys conform to the Establishment, from 1st May, 1699, to 1st December, 1700, being 19 months at £544 12s. monthly ; £10,347 8s.

Another paper, in less detail but in similar terms, is headed "The Lords Commissioners of the Treasury to Collonel James Ferguson's Regiment." It would seem, therefore, that if two companies were sent home in the previous year, they must have been disbanded, and the number was afterwards again raised to 12 or 13.

Before long there seems to have been another transference as far at least as pay was concerned. The Calendar of Treasury Papers contains the following entries :—

"Report of Mr. William Blaithwayt and Mr. W. Duncombe as to eight days' pay to Brigadier Ferguson and Col. Row for their regiments, due to them at the time they were sent from Scotland to Holland. Dated 23, March, 1703-4."

"Minuted 27 March 1704. D. Marlbro present. This canot be granted out of any of the English funds, these regiments being paid by English Mo. from ye very day of imbarcacon : but they are at libty. to apply to Scotl. where they should have been paid to their imbarcation."

It would seem that after their return to Scotland, the Cameronians were in great jeopardy of being disbanded. The correspondence addressed from Scotland to the politic Presbyterian ecclesiastic, who had the ear of King William, bears testimony to the anxiety felt by noblemen and others interested in the various regiments whose fate hung in the balance, when economy demanded a reduction of establishments. Among these letters to the future Principal Carstares, is one from Colonel Ferguson. It bears the stamp of the writer's individuality, and shews that he was a politician as well as a soldier, and sufficiently versed in the classics to be stung by lampoons in the dead languages levelled at the master whom he served. The time was a critical one; the heats of the Darien controversy were skilfully fomented by the Jacobites, the popular mind was fiercely excited, and the national spirit of hostility to the "auld enemies of England" was fanned for ulterior ends by those who had other objects to promote. The ferment had taken a direction very dangerous to the Government; they knew that in the North-Eastern Shires they had not above four or five friends to the New Establishment in each County, and in a wild tumult the Edinburgh mob broke loose, threatened the lives of those who had roused their anger, and rioted to the tune of "Wilful Willie." So the situation gave force to their Colonel's appeal on behalf of the Cameronians, who were certainly the Prœtorian Guard of Revolution principles north of the Tweed. On June 15th, 1700, he wrote thus to Mr. Carstares:—

"Dear Sir,—Since you went from this, things are grown rather worse than better : the ferment still continues, and new addresses are daily coming in from all parts of the country to be presented to the Parliament when they sit. God help us, we are ripening for destruction. It looks very like Forty-one. Yesterday, there came an address from the town of Glasgow to Powhill, their representative. Its much of the same nature with the rest ; for redressing of grievances, a legal settlement of our company in Darien, and to be eased of all subsidies and taxes. There are likewise some officers who have been desiring the army to address for their arrears. You see, sir, what kind of people we are, and how the King, our master, is served by us. But, God be thanked, there are more honest men amongst us than knaves. So I hope there will be no address from the army at this time. Monday last was a great day among the Jacobites here, being the birthday of the pretended Prince of Wales; and it was solemnised by a great many this year, who never did it before. I send a poem upon it, made by Dr. Pitcairn. Its an allusion to that fable in Aesop of the frogs desiring a King from Jupiter, who gave them a stork. There are a great many satyrical and obscene reflections upon the King in it.* You see, sir, that they are now above board with us; for treason is became so common that nobody takes any notice of it. They talk publicly that, unless the King will grant them the legal settlement of Caledonia, that they will address him again with forty thousand hands at it, and call a convention of States. We are all in flame; and I am sure the fuel comes both from France and England to keep it up. The Lord preserve our master and counsell from ought; and let all his enemies be confounded from Dan to Beersheba. I think, sir, you are very happy and safe where you are; but upon my word, I am not where I am, nor no honest man. If our master be necessitate to break some regiments, I hope he will have a regard to his old servants; for there are four or five younger than that which I have the honour to command, viz., Portmore's, Strathnaver's, Hamilton's, Maitland's, and Jedburgh's dragoons; for we were upon the Scots establishment before any of them. Besides, sir, we have our good service to plead for us; and that we have been honest and loyal from the beginning, and will continue so to the end. Pray give my most humble duty and service to our noble friend and patron. I have writ to him since you went from this. I hope he will continue his protection and favour to us; for we never will, nor ever did depend upon any but him, whom I pray God may long preserve.—Adieu."

It is interesting to find a strong supporter of the Government of William of Orange going back for a parallel to the existing excitement to the popular ferment that preceded the calamitous era of the Civil Wars. The observation, "it looks very like Forty-One," was probably accompanied by the recollection of how a year or two later that "Cavalier of stainless faith and purity," the Marquis of Huntly, had stepped from the writer's father's door to raise the Royal Standard in the little market-place of Inverurie. "Our noble friend and patron" was probably the Marquis of Douglas, the father of the young Colonel who had fallen at Steinkirk, or possibly the Duke of Queensberry, for the Cameronian Regiment was always associated with the Douglas name, and still bears on its appointments the mullet which was the badge of the most famous of Scottish Houses.

* Appendix V.

With the new century a new scene opened. In February, 1702, "Colonel Ferguson's regiment of foot was ordered immediately from Scotland to Holland." Next year we meet with him as Brigadier-General, holding a command at Bois-le-Duc, an important fortress in Dutch Brabant. There occurred there a very curious incident which must be told in the words of the individual principally concerned. The notorious Simon Fraser, afterwards Lord Lovat, in the course of the mysterious intrigues he had been for some time carrying on, which perplexed the Courts both of St. James and St. Germains, and procured him a lodging in the Bastile from the most Christian King, had made the acquaintance of Ferguson the Plotter in London. They had, according to Lovat, whose word always requires to be taken with reservation, and is often absolutely unreliable—deep conferences on the prospects of King James. But "the old Plotter," who had, if not more natural talent for intrigue than Lovat, at least at that time more experience in the art, suspected his associate of being more intent on gratifying his private hatreds than advancing the Jacobite cause. He gradually unravelled the tortuous thread of a conspiracy to ruin the Duke of Athole, by the disclosure of which at the right time he managed both to spoil a very pretty piece of mischief and throw discredit on the existence of the alleged Jacobite design known as "the Scots Plot." Before, however, the unravelling process had been quite completed, the intriguers "parted with mutual protestations of friendship and esteem," and Ferguson gave Fraser "a letter of recommendation to his brother, Major-General Ferguson, who had entered into the service of King William, and at that time commanded the Scottish regiments in garrison at Bois-le-Duc, entreating him to render the same services to Lord Lovat as he would to himself in his situation. This letter was the means of saving Lord Lovat's life about a fortnight after." He was travelling through Holland, and being a suspected person, found himself in great danger among the Dutch. " In this situation," he says, "he recollected the letter he had received from old Mr. Ferguson at London to Major General Ferguson, his brother, who commanded the troops at Bois-le-Duc. With this recommendation he determined to set out for that fortress ; himself, his brother, and Major Fraser, having disguised themselves in the uniform of Dutch officers." Having arrived there, "in the evening he waited upon General Ferguson, who having read his brother's letter, entreating him to communicate to Lord Lovat everything he knew respecting the interests of the King, and to bestow upon him all the attentions in his power, desired that nobleman to sup with him alone, observing that he could inform him of several things of the last importance to the two Courts. When Lord Lovat waited upon him in pursuance of his invitation the General assured him that, though he had been obliged for subsistence to enter into the service of King William and the Dutch Republic, he had always been in his heart faithfully attached to King James. He said that he should be charmed to meet with a favourable occasion of shedding his blood for the restoration of his prince. The more unquestionably to prove his zeal for this interest, he gave Lord Lovat a copy of the secret intelligence that M. Ivoye, at that time governor of Bois-le-Duc and a general officer of the Dutch artillery, had received from the secretaries of M. Chamillard, the French Minister for the War Department. In these letters all the designs of France respecting Spain, Flanders, and the other countries that were the seat of war, were detailed: designs which the King of France conceived to be unknown to any person beside his minister and favourite, M. Chamillard. This statesman, under the influence of a weakness fatal to his country, discovered them to his secretaries, who sold them again to the enemies of the King; and M. Ivoye had a round sum of money from the States of Holland for this business. It is indeed notorious, that this infamous traffic was carried on with more success under the administration of M. Chamillard than it had ever been before; it being extremely rare for Frenchmen to betray the interests of their monarch. Lord Lovat stayed with General Ferguson till after midnight: and the General told him that he would send his valet-de-chambre to introduce him again the next day by a private door.

"In the morning, however, the commander found his garrison alarmed and mutinous. Some officers of the regiments of Orkney and Murray, relations and friends of Lord Athole, understood that Lord Lovat was in the town and had been addressed by several soldiers of the Fraser Clan, who were enlisted in their regiments. These gentlemen immediately spread a report, that he was come thither to debauch the Scottish garrison and induce them to desert. The officers in general had heard this report and represented it to their commander, desiring him to arrest Lord Lovat as an enemy to the State, and a partizan and emissary of France.

"Upon this event General Ferguson despatched immediately a message to bring Lord Lovat incognito to his head quarters. He told him, with concern the great danger in which he was: that it was necessary he should disguise himself and set out upon the spot, since if the Dutch had the least rumour of the intelligence which had been spread by the Scottish officers it would be impossible for him to save his life, or hinder him from being cut into a thousand pieces. Lord Lovat thanked General Ferguson with great warmth, and told him that he was ready to set out instantly, provided he had the means of arriving in safety at Antwerp.

The affair was difficult, but Mr. Ferguson accomplished it by means of a sum of money, and by the assistance of a rich Dutch Roman Catholic merchant, whom he knew to be deeply attached to the French interest. This merchant brought to Mr. Ferguson and Lord Lovat a Catholic Postilion, whom he used when he went to Antwerp and Brussels in time of peace. The postilion had three saddle and one draught horse. He agreed to conduct Lord Lovat and his brother to Antwerp upon two of the saddle-horses, himself being mounted on the third; offering his little cart to convey Major Fraser and Lord Lovat's page. At the same time he demanded 100 louisd'or upon the spot in ready money, for the risk of his horses, and 50 for the risk of his life, both of them being forfeited in case of a discovery. Lord Lovat counted down the sum required, and, by the advice of Mr. Ferguson, disguised himself like a carter, in order to drive the cart out of the town. In this disguise he passed all the gates and redoubts of Bois-le-Duc."

Such is the story told by Lord Lovat in his Memoirs. It is a curious one, and scarcely consistent, in some of its details, with the career we have been tracing, or with the tradition of Brigadier Ferguson's family, which always represented him as a strong supporter of King William and the Protestant succession. When we are astonished by finding the commander of the Cameronians depicted as a Jacobite in disguise, we feel inclined to ask for more reliable testimony than the word of Lord Lovat, and remembering the confident opinions of General Mackay and Captain Pottinger, already quoted, as to his being "a man of probity and honour"—and old Mackay was well qualified to judge of probity—"faithful and enthusiastic in the service of King William," "vigorous and well affected," "of great diligence and zealously affected to the present Government"—we seek for some other explanation of the hospitality afforded to the fugitive than is given in the confession, which he describes as made to him. Nor is such difficult to discover. Apart from the natural feeling which would influence the General to protect "a kindly Scot" from the fury of the Dutch, there would be the desire to oblige his brother, and in the state of public affairs at the time, it was a much more grateful service to the Government to get a political busybody well away quietly, than to embarrass the Ministry with a State-trial. For during the reign of Anne, "a Stuart, yet Protestant, and prosperous," there was a tendency to treat the Jacobites leniently, and to regard their operations with half-closed eyes, until they became really serious, and it was the sudden resort to the opposite policy, with the triumph of the Whigs on her death, which precipitated the outbreak of 1715, and, in Bolingbroke's words, "dyed the royal ermines of a prince, no way sanguinary, in blood." It is possible that Ferguson, like the great chief under whom he served, and many others, whose politics had been Tory though not Jacobite, having acted zealously in the Revolution, and having, unlike Marlborough, served King William faithfully, had never wholly put out of sight the ultimate restoration of the old line under conditions securing the safety of the Protestant religion. We can well believe, that to him the words of the old Covenanter at Dunse Law would have powerfully appealed—" We desyred but to keep our own in the service of our prince, as our ancestors had done; we loved no new masters. Had our throne been voyd, and our voyces sought for the filling of Fergus's chaire, we would have died ere any other had sitten down on that fatall marble but Charles alone."

There is an inherent improbability in one whose fidelity was not above suspicion being selected for such enterprises as he had been entrusted with in Scotland, or charged with the duties he is soon after found performing in the great campaign, which is strengthened by the conduct of his captors in 1689, and his own in 1690, while the articles under which the Cameronian regiment had been embodied stipulated "that all the officers of the regiment shall be such as in conscience and prudence, may with cordial confidence be submitted unto and followed"—"well affected, of approven fidelity, and of a sober conversation." Lovat, in describing his contemporaries, is always "over-violent or over-civil," and the strain of affectation which led him to pose as a classic patriot on the scaffold, inspires him to speak of transactions no better or worse than his own in language of elevated praise or equally eloquent abuse. At this time a Jacobite plotter realized to his mind the ideal of heroic virtue, and to describe an acquaintance as such was probably intended as a high compliment. Certainly the sentences in which he speaks of Ferguson as "faithfully attached to King James," and "charmed to meet with a favourable occasion of shedding his blood for the restoration of his Prince," have much more the ring of his peculiar personality, than of one who had been the trusted subordinate of Mackay, and friendly correspondent of Carstares, and was the superior of Blackader. They are far from harmonising with one or two references in a curious manuscript Memoir, written 40 years later by the daughter-in-law of Brigadier Ferguson, a lady whose sentiments may easily be gathered from a sentence in a letter written in 1746,* in which a clerical gentleman reminds his correspondent—"if you have any letters for Old Deer † remember that the Lady Kinmundy hath given it the name of Dear William." It does not appear whether this remarkable, but fortunately evanescent designation was bestowed in honour of William of Orange or the Duke of Cumberland. The Lady Kinmundy refers with satisfaction to the fact that her husband's brother, "alone of all his father's family had been honoured to set up his standard about God's Tabernacle, I mean the Church of Scotland," and "died a standard-bearer for the Protestant religion in the late French War, and was honoured to come over with our blessed deliverer, King

---

* Printed in one of the Spalding Club Publications.
† Old Deer was then included in the estate of Kinmundy.

William." That the General talked politics in a guarded manner with an embarrassing guest, whose departure he was zealous in expediting is probable, and that Lovat misconceived or misrepresented the tenor of what passed is likely enough, but it does not appear that Fraser ever made any use in France of the information he says he received, and, even assuming the terms of the introduction to be correctly stated, it may be questioned whether they imported a very high degree of confidence. We may safely conclude that the effect of the General's wine had been to quicken Lord Lovat's always lively imagination, and that he romanced at length upon the foundation of a little Scottish hospitality in a foreign land. It is perhaps a coincidence worthy of notice that, when in 1746, Lovat was seized hiding in a hollow tree on an island in Loch Morar, by a party of sailors from the Furnace and Campbell Militia, the naval part of the force was commanded by a grand-nephew of the General who had entertained him at Bois-le-Duc. He met with less courtesy now, for as the sailors marched him off to the ship, the pipers of the Campbells played the Lovat March.

III.

BRIGADIER AT BLENHEIM.

"Malbrook s'en va t'en guerre."
—*French air.*

"IF there be," said Lord Beaconsfield, "any epoch of history more glorious, more satisfactory than another, it is the reign of Queen Anne. Then were our armies most brilliant with success, then were our victories most glorious; for even Waterloo, the most famed of battles, has not obliterated the memory of Blenheim." And the high authority of Canning not only illustrates the reverence with which the men of a truly great time regard the past, but claims respect for the opinion that the reigns of William and Anne were "the best times of our history." Certainly the year 1704 was one of the most stirring in the annals of Great Britain, for there were all the elements which impress the mind in the contest she was carrying on. The scene of conflict was classic ground in military annals, and its fame "blazed broader yet in after years," yet the strife was to extend from the "Lowlands of Holland" to "Hic Germanie;" the forces were vast, and wielded by rare genius; and the adversary was that "old France," at once so chivalrous and mighty, then at the height of her power and prestige. The ostensible cause was the question "to which lion's paw," the Spanish Succession was to fall, but the real interests at stake in the earlier years of the war, were the Protestant Religion and the Balance of Power. It was one of "those great conjunctures which call all the principal powers of the Continent into the field," and in Marlborough and Prince Eugene, its issue was to be determined by men equal to the occasion. Hitherto the war had dragged on without any decisive achievements, but now the crisis was at hand.

The "Grand Monarque" had developed his great scheme for striking at the heart of the Empire, and Marlborough had resolved on a decisive effort to meet it, on which hung the fate of the civilised world. The English Cabinet had been re-organised by the admission of Harley and St. John; and in the spring Marlborough had set his troops in motion for that march to the Moselle, which was not to terminate till he had ascended the Rhine, and driven the veterans of France fugitives into the Danube.

Throughout this campaign the Duke seems to have relied greatly on the experience and energy of Brigadier Ferguson, whenever there was special work to be done. He was to commit the care of his base and the defence of the line of the Meuse and the Low Countries to Dutch troops, and desired to review these forces in a body before finally embarking on his great enterprise. It was, therefore, necessary to temporarily supply their places in the garrisons, and especially at Maestricht, with British troops, and for this purpose, a body of four thousand men was ordered out of the several British garrisons in Holland in the beginning of March. A Journal of the campaign has preserved the exact route followed by this force, and the name of the officer to whom the command was entrusted. On the 9th of March "all the detachments, from their several garrisons, joined at the Bosch, under the Honourable Brigadier Ferguson's command.

10th—The Brigadier, with the said command, marched from the Bosch to, and cantoned in Osch, four leagues.

11th—Marched from Osch village to, and cantoned in the village of Wanray, five leagues.

12th—Marched from Wanray to, and cantoned in Grounock village, four leagues.

14th—Marched from Grounock to, and cantoned in Griffen-Swaert, on the west side of the Maes, near unto Venlo; and the next day crossed the Maes early in the morning, and marched thence thro' Roermonde to, and cantoned in and about the village of Harten (five leagues), a little southward from Roermonde; where the Brigadier left Major Cornwallis with a reinforcement of nine hundred men, being the detachment of three Battalions.

March 16th—The Brigadier, with the rest, marched from Hart to, and cantoned in Spaubeck—six leagues.

17th—Marched from Spaubeck into, and reinforced Maestricht—three leagues. This journey contains about thirty-nine leagues.

21st—The Holland's garrison marched out of Maestricht, and left the keeping thereof to Brigadier Ferguson with the English detachment, and joined a great body of their own and auxiliary troops on Peter's Hill on the west side of the town."

For about five weeks, Ferguson seems to have commanded the garrison of Maestricht, and they must have been weeks full of occupation.

The Duke of Marlborough "reached Maestricht," says his biographer Archdeacon Cox, " on the 10th of May. Here he continued till the 14th actively employed in assembling and organizing the army, superintending the formation of magazines, and pressing the march of the troops to the place of rendezvous." On the 11th he reviewed the army, and the same day he wrote to the future Bolingbroke. "On Wednesday next they pass the Meuse at Ruremond on their march towards the Moselle, and I may venture to tell you (though I would not have it public as yet) I design to march a great deal higher into Germany." The quaint old town of Maestricht, with its spacious market places, and high sloping roofs, must then have been a busy place with troops marching, ammunition trains being despatched, and the conviction in the minds of all which the arrival of "the Great Captain" inspired, that a great enterprise was about to be entered on. Those who reflected on what lay before them, must have felt that if a splendid opportunity awaited them, they were also going to encounter great peril, and little as was known of the ultimate aim of the General, it was evident that the result of the campaign just opening must be either unequalled triumph or complete disaster. The military ascendancy of France in Europe had been for years unquestioned, and the prestige of the French soldiery was yet unbroken. The circumstances of 1704, were perhaps most nearly paralleled when the British infantry, under Sir John Stuart, gave the first check to the legions of Napoleonic France on the field of Maida, in 1806, but Blenheim was to be the Maida and Waterloo of that war in one. The British had, it is true, fought with stubborn gallantry in the previous war amid the slaughter of Steinkirk and the carnage of Landen, and drawn from the reserved

William the exclamation "See my brave English," but in both these battles the victory had been to the French, and they might have pointed to that practical demonstration which Marlborough was soon to cite to Tallard, which gives the pre-eminence over even "the best troops in Europe" to *ceux qui les ont battus*. And whatever reliance their own commanders might place on the mettle of the British troops, the bulk of the confederate army was composed of allies and auxiliaries. Had it been a question of reckoning probabilities, the odds would have been given largely in favour of France, and for those about to march under Marlborough's command, the occasion, if a very stirring, was also a solemn one. The bare dates even of musty documents become instinct with life, and even private papers of trivial importance have some public interest, when they speak of exciting surroundings and an important moment. It is therefore not uninteresting to notice that Brigadier Ferguson, amid all the bustle of preparation for the march, found time to review and regulate his private affairs, and settle their disposal in the event of his falling in the battles about to be fought. "At Maestricht, the 12th day of May, 1704," is the place and date of a settlement of accounts between him and his nephew, Mr. James Ferguson of Pitfour, an advocate at the Scots bar, who managed his affairs in Scotland for him. It would seem as if the constant occupation involved in preparing his command efficiently for the campaign had rendered it necessary to delay finally setting in order his personal concerns, till the moment of leisure which often intervenes at the last between the completion of preparation and the commencement of action. His will bears the same date, and purports to have been written by Mr. James Ferguson, advocate, but if the frame of the bequeathing clauses evidences the nephew's legal knowledge, the introductory sentences may perhaps be taken as preserving no mere words of style, but as showing the hand of the Commander of the Cameronians himself. "Many a trait of character," writes the noble and cultured author of the "Lives of the Lindsays," "may be read in the language and provisions of a will of the olden time," and "these intimations, so gratifying to posterity," are in this case at least characteristic of the time and the man:—"Be it known to all men be thes present letters, me Brigadier James ffergusone of Bomakellie, forasmuch as noe thing is more certain as death, nor more uncertaine as the time and manner thereof, And I being most earnest and desireous to leave my worldly affaires cleare where ever it pleases God to remove me from this transitory life, And being at present in perfect health of Body, and soundness in minde, Doe therefore make this my Latter Will and Testament as after follows (to wit), I bequeath my Soul to God Allmighty to be saved by the allone merits of his only son, and my Lord and Redeemer, and I recommend my body to be decently and honourably Interred where it pleases God to call me. And for my worldly affaires and substance I dispose of them in manner following &c." Two days later the Bulletin, dated Maestricht, 14th May, 1704, contained the announcement :— " Our detachment under the command of Brigadier Ferguson will march from hence tomorrow, and my Lord Duke of Marlborough having concerted measures with the generals here will follow on Friday, and on Sunday we shall join all the English troops at Bedburg, near Cologne, and so pursue our march towards Coblenz." On the Friday evening Marlborough caught up Ferguson's detachment, and marched with them from near Linnick to Bedburg where they joined the English forces and train of artillery under General Churchill.

Brigadier Ferguson's command was composed of a battalion of the First Guards (Grenadiers), a battalion of Orkney's Regiment (the 1st of the Line or Royal Scots), and Ingoldsby's (the 23rd or Welsh Fusiliers). It was a fine brigade, and bore the brunt of the fighting in the operations that followed, for it led and sustained the attack on the Schellenberg, and at Blenheim shared with Rowe's Brigade the protracted struggle round the strongest part of the French position. Without delay Marlborough pressed forward the execution of his grand design. From Bonn, marching early in the morning, and resting during the heat of the day, he proceeded up the left bank of the Rhine, "the stores and sick being sent up the river in boats, the men marching along joyously, quenching their thirst in Rhenish wines." At Coblentz he crossed the river, and advanced to Mayence, where the army was reviewed before the Elector, who was so much struck with the appearance of the troops that, alluding to an entertainment to be given in the evening to the officers, he remarked, "These gentlemen appear to be all dressed for the ball." At last, at the end of June, the allied army found itself in front of the fortified height of Schellenberg, the key of Donauwerth, which they were anxious to secure as a *place d'armes* for the invasion of Bavaria. This position, strong by nature, and strengthened by art, was occupied by a Gallo-Bavarian force of 12000 men, whose right rested on the Danube and their left on the covered way of Donauwerth, while a line of entrenchments, uncompleted but formidable, ran along their front. Marlborough determined to lose no time in attacking, and, without waiting for the arrival of the main body of the Imperialists, selected a picked body of 6000 foot, to lead the asault. They were supported by 30 squadrons, and three battalions of Austrian Grenadiers on the right. A forlorn hope of 50 Grenadiers of the English Guards, led by Lord Mordaunt, (of whom only ten, besides himself, came out of the action,) preceded them, and at six o'clock in the evening of the 2nd July, "they proceeded upon the attack, Brigadier Ferguson leading up the first line of foot, Count Horn and the other Generals bringing up the rest : Lieutenant-General Goor commanding the whole." They pressed forward exposed to a storm of grape from the entrenchments in front, and a flanking fire from the works of Donauwerth, and as they got nearer, the the enemy loaded with case which did "very great execution." The first discharge of musketry struck down General Goor, and many other officers, and an unfortunate error by which the men mistook a ravine they had to cross for the ditch of the entrenchment, and flung in their fascines, caused a momentary hesitation. The enemy then "came out of their trenches with bayonets in their pieces, but they were quickly obliged to return to them again," for the Guards stood their ground bravely, and the rest of Ferguson's Brigade "coming up at this critical moment rushed forward to their support." But though the enemy were driven back into their lines, these were not yet won, and the defence was so vigorous that the assailants were twice repulsed, and the carnage was great. Then Lord John Hay dismounted his dragoons (the Scots Greys), and brought them up to the aid of the infantry, and the Imperialists forcing an entrance where the lines had been denuded of their defenders, called to meet the principal attack, the whole pressed forward, the entrenchment was carried, and the enemy fled in confusion. "The Duke of Marlborough coming in with the first of our squadrons, found our foot pursuing the enemy, and, therefore, ordered Brigadier Ferguson to keep them to their colours and continue upon the field of battle, whilst he made a clear stage of the enemy with the horse only."

In this action, which Marlborough described as "the warmest that has been known for many years," and Blackader in his diary, as "one of the hottest I have seen," the regiments composing Ferguson's Brigade "suffered more than any others." Of his own regiment, the Cameronians, apparently not in his own brigade, only a detachment of 130 men were engaged; of its officers, Capt. Lawson and Lieut. Seaton were wounded, and it lost one Sergeant and 18 privates killed, and three Sergeants and fifty-seven Privates wounded. The victory was complete, though its lustre soon paled before that of Blenheim; and the Emperor, conscious that it had saved the House of Austria, might well write to Marlborough— "This will be an eternal trophy to your most serene Queen in Upper Germany, whither the victorious arms of the English Nation have never penetrated since the memory of man."

A month passed in marches, negotiations, and laying waste the lands of the Elector of Bavaria; and again on the 12th of August, the combined troops of Marlborough and Eugene, confronted the united forces of Marshall Tallard and the Elector. The allied Generals on that morning advanced, accompanied by the battalion of Guards from Ferguson's Brigade, of which Marlborough was himself Colonel, and from the Tower of Dapfheim Church, observed the Quarter-Masters of the Gallo-Bavarian army marking out their camp on the rising ground beyond the Nebel. They then returned to the camp of their own army behind the Kessel, and made preparations for attacking the enemy the next day. The French and Bavarian army, largely outnumbering the allies, stretched from the Danube, on which their right rested, to the high ground, bounding on the north the valley through which it flowed, and as the river was nowhere fordable, they could only be attacked in front. The steep banks and marshy bottom through which the Nebel flowed down to the Danube presented an obstacle to the assailants, and several villages lent additional strength to the defence. Of these, the most important was Blenheim, on the right of the French position, and the advantages afforded by the houses and garden walls were increased by the construction of entrenchments, barricades, and palisades. It was occupied by a force of twenty-two battalions and six squadrons of the *élite* of the French army, supported by artillery, which swept the approaches, and was regarded by Tallard as the most important part of his line. Indeed, his throwing so many men into Blenheim, by weakening his centre, largely contributed to lose him the battle, but it very much increased the difficulty and danger of the task allotted to the brigades directed against the village.

The British army moved forward from their encampment early in the morning of the 13th, and picking up the force under Major-General Wilkes, which had been pushed forward the day before to secure the pass of Dapfheim, advanced in nine columns, and deployed into order of battle about seven o'clock. Lord Cutts had command of the ninth column, "upon the left of all by itself next the Danube," composed of Rowes' and Ferguson's British brigades, Hulsen's Hessian infantry, and the British cavalry under Wood and Ross. "Lord Cutts had orders with these troops to attack the village of Blenheim."

Marlborough's attack was delayed by the time required by Prince Eugene's forces to come into line of battle on the right. Divine service was performed by the chaplains at the head of each regiment, and Marlborongh was "observed to join with peculiar fervour in this solemn appeal to the Giver of Victory." He then rode along the lines to find his troops impatient for the signal, narrowly escaping a French cannon ball which passed beneath his charger and covered him with earth. Under a heavy artillery fire, the British soldiers established six bridges over the Nebel. At last, about mid-day, hearing that Prince Eugene was ready, Marlborough ordered Lord Cutts to begin the attack on Blenheim. His troops, descending to the Nebel, took possession of two water mills on its banks under a heavy fire of grape, and continued their advance up the slope, receiving the first small-arm discharge of the enemy at thirty paces. Rowe, whose brigade was leading, struck his sword into the palisades before he gave the order to fire, but in a few minutes he fell mortally wounded; his Lieutenant-Colonel and Major were killed trying to carry him off; one-third of his men had dropped, and the brigade shattered and disordered, fell back on the Hessians. "The enemy," says Cox, "having placed four additional pieces of artillery upon the height near Blenheim, swept the fords of the Nebel with grapeshot. But, notwithstanding this destructive fire, the brigades of Ferguson and Hulsen crossed near the lower watermill, and advanced in front of the village. The enemy therefore withdrew the guns within their defences and met the attack with such vigour that, after three successive repulses, the assailants halted under cover of the rising ground." "Whilst Row's brigade," writes Lediard, "rallied themselves, that of Ferguson commanded by himself attacked the village of Blenheim on the left, but with no better success; and though both returned three or four times to the charge, with equal vigour, yet were they both still repulsed with like disadvantage, so that it was found impossible to force the enemy in that post without entirely sacrificing the infantry."

General Sir Frederick Hamilton thus describes the nature of the deadly combat in which those troops were engaged:—"Upon Rowe's and Ferguson's Brigades crossing the Nebel, they halted under cover of the bank to reform. The First Guards, under Colonel Philip Dormer, were on the right of Ferguson's Brigade, and as they ascended the ridge which at first concealed them from the view of the troops in Blenheim, they found themselves opposite the centre of that village exposed to the direct musketry fire of its garrison. The soldiers, reserving their fire, steadily advanced in the most intrepid manner towards the palisades by which it was defended, but a deadly volley at thirty paces distant struck down many a gallant fellow, while the rest rushing forward attempted by sheer strength to drag away the palings; they fired through the intervals, or struck at the Frenchmen with their swords and clubbed muskets wherever an opportunity offered itself; but all efforts were unavailing. Dormer commanding the battalion was killed: Mordaunt lost an arm: and young Campion, one of the ensigns, was desperately wounded in the nearly successful attempt to pull away the wooden barrier." The French cavalry charged the right of Rowe's disordered troops, and were in turn charged by the British horse, who, coming under the fire of Blenheim, fell back behind the Hessians. "In the meantime, Ferguson's Brigade with the First Guards, already much reduced by their gallant attack at Schellenberg, and by the stubborn resistance of the garrison of Blenheim, assisted now by the Hanoverians, renewed their attempt upon that village, but without cannon to breach the palisading, their efforts were again unavailing, and they stood exposed to the murderous fire of the garrison, until Marlborough, who had not been previously aware of the extraordinary strength of the post, desired Lord Cutts to withdraw for a time under the shelter of the rising ground."

Baffled though they were in their endeavours to force an entrance, the troops of Lord Cutts held the ground they had won, and kept the twenty-two battalions occupying Blenheim employed until the battle was decided elsewhere, and it was from the tenacity with which he stood his ground in front of the village, in spite of the storm of bullets that came from it, that Lord Cutts received the designation of "the Salamander that lives in fire." After the French centre had been driven off the field in confusion, the veterans posted in Blenheim maintained their own, and as they were many in numbers, and in a very strong position, the task in which Lord Cutts had failed, seemed no easy one for the whole Allied Army. General Churchill took post in rear of the village, resting his right on the Danube, Lord Orkney approached from the north, while Lord Cutts, again advancing with Ferguson's and Rowe's Brigades, threatened it from the side of the Nebel. For some time there was sharp fighting, but it was the interest of both sides to put a stop to a struggle which might be bloody for the victors, and must be fruitless on the part of the vanquished. The French proposed to capitulate, but General Churchill insisted on unconditional surrender. "No resource remained: to resist was hopeless, to escape impossible. With despair and indignation the troops submitted to their fate, and the regiment of Navarre in particular burnt their colours, and buried their arms, that such trophies might not remain to grace the triumph of an enemy. Twenty-four battalions and twelve squadrons, surrendered themselves prisoners of war; and thus closed the mighty struggle of this eventful day."

"'The trophies of this victory," says General Hamilton, "which saved the Austrian Empire, and for the time destroyed the power of France in central Europe, consisted of 100 guns, 24 mortars, 129 colours, 171 standards, 17 pair of kettledrums, 3600 tents &c. &c. The loss of the enemy in men was also very great, and the number of prisoners and deserters raised their total casualties to more than 40,000 men before the dispirited remains of the French army reached Strasbourg." The victorious army bivouacked on the field of battle, and the weary troops, who had accomplished the march of the morning, and sustained the stress of the struggle round the village, forming a hollow square round the great crowd of prisoners "continued on their arms all night to secure them." Lediard, after mentioning the officers of higher rank who specially distinguished themselves, adds, "and Row, Ferguson, and Bernsdorff, Brigadiers of Foot, deserve particularly to be mentioned, for their great bravery and prudent conduct," and Oldmixon includes Ferguson in a similar list of those "whose names ought to live with honour as long as history can preserve them."

Though not forming part of the brigade he commanded, Ferguson's own regiment was hotly engaged, and interesting information as to its fortunes in the battle is afforded by a document headed "A State of the Respective Companys of the Regiment under the command of Brigadier James Ferguson after the battle of Blenheim, distinguishing the commission officers that were killed, wounded, or absent by sickness or order, and the non-commission that were killed, wounded, or absent by sickness or order, and the non-commission officers and soldiers that were disabled. As also an account of the widows and children of such officers as were killed." Among the officers the casualties were heavy. Those present after the battle were, Colonel and Captain Brigadier Ferguson, Lieutenant-Colonel and Captain Livingston, Major and Captain Borthwick, Captain Cranston of the Grenadier Company, Captains Blackader, Munro, and Drummond, Lieutenants Dickson, Wilson, Douglas, Lindsay, John Ferguson, Bernard, Weems, and Ensigns Simpson, Dalrymple, Oliphant, Marshall, and Ogilvie, with the following staff-officers:— Adjutant Forge (?) Quarter-Master Stevenson, Surgeons Stewart and Man, and Chaplain Pitcairn. There were wounded Lieut.-Colonel Livingston, Captain Blackader, Captain Borthwick, Captain Lawson (hit at Schellenberg) and Captain

Wilson, Lieutenants Robert Ferguson, Wilson, Leonard Ferguson, and Ensigns Dalrymple, Oliphant, Marshall, and Ogilvie, and Quarter-Master Stevenson. Absent on order were Major Borthwick, Captain Aikman, Lieutenant Drummond and Ensign Morris, and through sickness Captain Hamilton and Ensign Gray. Killed on the spot were Captains Campbell and Stewart, Lieutenants Seaton, Moncrief, and Douglas; Ensigns Hay, Bernard, Low, Maclain and Balfour. Seaton left a widow and three children, Moncrief a widow and one child, and Hay and Bernard each a widow. One sergeant and two corporals out of 34 sergeants and 33 corporals were disabled. There had been present before the battle 24 drummers, and 538 private soldiers, and the column which records the losses is unfortunately mutilated, so that it is only possible to read the first two figures which are 16. The paper which seems to have been an exact copy of the return actually sent in, is docquetted "London,—of feby.,—170¼, this is a true state of my regt. after the battle of Hoghstate.—Ja. Ferguson."

Another document entitled "The State of the Honorable Brigadier Ffergusone's Regt. after the two actions in Germanie, 1704," gives a complete roll of each company signed by "the commanding officer present with each company."* There were 13 companies, but one only mustered 20 rank and file, and the strongest 46. The state of the Brigadier's own company is signed by his subaltern, "Rot· ffergusone"; and the whole was "justified and attested" as "just and conform to the state of the regiment," by himself, at the Bosch, in April, 1705. The names of the officers speak for themselves, and from those of the rank and file, there can be no doubt as to the thoroughly Scottish character of the regiment. There had been taken prisoners no less than 11,000 men, and on the night of the battle, "our regiment," says Blackader, "was one of those that guarded them." 5,678 were assigned to Marlborough as his share, and their disposal raised a question of some difficulty, on account of their numbers, and the want of a place to secure them. Brigadier Ferguson was finally detached with five British battalions, to march them to Mayence, and take them down the Rhine. The bulletin, dated

---

* This is in duplicate, one copy having the actual signatures.

camp at Weissembourg, 12th September, 1704, states—" Brig. Ferguson is marched this morning with five battalions of foot, viz., one of the royal regiment, (1st), General Churchill's, the Lord North and Grey's, Brig. Row's (21st Scots Fusiliers), and Brig. Meredyth's regiments for Mayence, where they are to embark with the French prisoners, and conduct them to Holland," and, on the 7th October, Marlborough wrote to the Brigadier, * ordering him to arrange for the disposal of the troops in the Dutch garrisons, with M. Slingelandt on behalf of the States. At Mayence, the Brigadier was joined by Captain Blackader, who had gone to the baths at Wiesbaden to recruit, and who now seems to have obtained from him the orders he had been hoping for, to go to Scotland in search of men to fill the vacancies caused by the campaign, as he accompanied him to Holland, and before long found he "was the first has yet reached Edinburgh, of any that were at the battles in Germany." At Nimeguen, the French prisoners were handed over to the Dutch authorities; three of the British regiments marched to Breda and two to Bois-le-Duc. The Brigadier probably accompanied the latter, for about Christmas time he was married at Bois-le-Duc to Hester Elizabeth, daughter of Herr Abraham Hibelet "*predicant van der Waalse Gemeente*" —*i.e.*, Pastor of the Walloon or Belgian Protestant church, there. Their marriage contract bears to have been signed "*binnen s' Hertogen-Bosch in huyse van de toekomende Bruyt's Vader op den*

---

* The Duke of Marlborough to Brigadier Ferguson.

Au camp de Weissembourg le 7 Octobre, 1704.
Monsieur,

MM. Les Etats ayant souhaités que les cinq bataillons qui sont partis d'ici avec vous, et quatre autres des troupes Anglaises qui doivent s'embarquer en peu de jours puissent être disposés dans les garnisons sélon la Memoire ci-joint, je vous prie de regler le tout avec M. Slingelandt comme il se trouvera le plus commode pour les troupes eu égard aux quartiers où les cinq bataillons seront à présent, et de donner ses ordes aux quatre bataillons qui viennent á Nimègue á l'avenant; en cas que nous n'en envoyions pas deux droit á Ruremonde, dont on aura soin de vous avertir. Et comme leurs H. P. pourraient encore demander trois des regiments qui ont resté tout cet été en garnison á Breda et Bois-le-Duc pour marcher á Maestricht, vous devez en ce cas donner les ordes á ceux qui sont dans le meilleur état de marcher deux de Breda, et un de Bois-le-Duc, selon les patentes quils recevront de M. M. les Etats.
Je suis Monsieur, &c., M.

ses en twintigste (26th) december, seventien hondert vier," and on the next day they were formally betrothed * in the "*groote kerk*," or beautiful cathedral of Bois-le-Duc. They must soon have made a hurried visit to England, possibly in time to share in the last of the great rejoicings for the victories, for the Brigadier signed papers in London in February, and his little children were sent up from Kirktonhill to meet him there.

In the campaign of 1705, in which the army acting on the Moselle experienced such hardships that "the Scots thought an army in their Highlands could shift better," and in which Marlborough performed the feat of forcing the French lines in Brabant, till then deemed impregnable, and nearly anticipated Wellington on the field of Waterloo,† Ferguson's brigade consisted

* I am indebted to the courtesy of M. Van der Does de Willebois, Burgomaster of Bois-le-duc in 1887, for extracts from the registers of that town authenticating the betrothal, and the baptism of a daughter in the following year. The first is in these terms—"Dat op den Zeven en twintigste der maand December Zeventein honderd vier alhier is onder trouwrd in de groote kerk de Herr Jacob Ferguson, weed ? (weduwenaar), Brigadier van de troupen van haer Majesteyt van groot Brittagne met Jufforouwe Hester Elizabeth Gibelet j.d. (jonge-dochter) van den Bosch, wonende in de nieuwstraat.

de tweede gebod opheden en het derde als toekomende Sondag te proclameren —den derden January, 1705."

The second is—

"Dat op den elfden (11th) der maand Octobre Zeventein honderd vyf alhier is gedoopt in de Waalsche kerk ; Anna Elizabeth née le 8 Octobre fille de Monsieur Jacob Ferguson Brigadier des troupes Angloises de sa Majesté Britannique et de Madame Hester Elizabeth Hibelet, aiant pour parain et pour maraine Monsieur et Madame Hibelet grand-père et grand-mère du susdit enfant."

† On 2nd January, 1705, the Duke of Marlborough wrote to Major-General Wood from St. James's. "Application has been made here by the States Minister, that you might, upon any extraordinary occasion, be ordered to furnish proportionable detachments out of the Queen's forces as the service should require, which, being already in the instructions you have received, I shall add nothing on that subject more than to desire you will take care to communicate the same to Brigadier Ferguson and to the several garrisons, that they may comply therewith, so as, however, to have all due regard to the preservation of the troops, it being not intended by this that they should change their quarters, but only send out detachments on any emergency. I must likewise desire you will inform the Brigadier, and the several regiments of foot at the same time, with her Majesty's pleasure, that they provide as little wheel baggage for the

of his own regiment, the Cameronians or 26th, the 16th, the 28th, and Stringer's, subsequently disbanded.

campaign as possible, concerning which you may expect a regulation by the next post."

The diary previously quoted mentions that, on April 20th, 1705, "Brigadier Ferguson, with the garrison of the Bosch, set out therefrom, all in great expedition, towards Maestricht, where our general rendezvous was intended," and tells how the Brigadier, picking up the garrisons of Venlo and Ruremonde, "passed Maestricht and pitched at Buzee village, on the west bank of the river Maes, halfway between Maestricht and Liége, somewhat apart from Holland army, in Marshal Overquerque's command, who had then joined and lay encamped on Peter's hill, near the citadel of Maestricht."

Captain Blackader's diary and letters, for 1705, contain the following:—
"April 12. Leaving Rotterdam and going up to the regiment: at night came into the Busse."

"April 17. Taken up all day in preparations for marching. More easy and composed this year in going out to the camp than the last."

"April 20. Marching out of the Busse."

"May 20-24. Marching every day. Walking alone and meditating along the banks of the Moselle. Drawing near the enemy and in prospect of fighting."

:"June 5. Getting account this day that we are to march back again, just down the same way we came up."

"June 21. Crossing the Maese. This day has been a fatiguing long march, continuing from three in the morning till eleven at night. A great many of the army fell by with weariness and some died, it being a scorching hot day."

"July 6. When I came home I found that our regiment and the whole army had orders to march immediately. We guessed it was to attack the French lines; accordingly we marched at nine o'clock at night in great silence, and marched all night. . . . . July 7. We attacked the French lines this morning, and got in much easier and cheaper than we expected. The lines were partly forced and partly surprised, for the French had a part of their army there, but not sufficient to make head against us; not knowing that we were to attack them at that place; for there was a feint made to attack them in another part, which made them draw their forces that way. Our horse had some action with them, and beat them wherever they encountered them. Our foot had nothing to do, for the enemy fled before they came up."

"July 9. Resting this day over against the enemy. The town (Louvain) between us, which is firing upon us, and some of the bullets coming in among our tents, but little harm done."

"July 23. I observe this, all this campaign, that, in all skirmishes between us and them, it appears we are masters of them, and could beat them as easy as a mastiff worries a cur-dog; but at the same time I observe that we are, as it were, chained down, and cannot get them soundly beat. It is currently believed here that, both at the lines and now, it is the States and their

He was not destined to share in the future triumphs of Ramilies and Oudenarde, for he died very suddenly at Bois-le-Duc on the 22nd October, 1705, a few days after the birth of his daughter. The tradition of his family attributes his death to poison. "He served," are the old-fashioned words of an old *MS.*, "in four reigns, still maintaining the character of a brave, valiant, and prudent officer, until his fame raising envy in the breast of the then commanding officer, he was cut off by very sinister means." An entry in the diary which Colonel Blackader, to the mortification of the historical student, devoted rather to the record of his own personal religious experiences than the interesting events amid which he lived, illustrates how great a shock the news was to his friends:—"I got the surprising account of our Brigadier's death, with which I was greatly affected. *Man's breath goeth out, to earth he turns, that day his thoughts perish.* O the vanity of human grandeur! He was just come from court, where he was sent for that he might be raised a step higher for his services." In accounts connected with the funeral, and letters written afterwards, he is described as Major-General, and his name appears among the Major-Generals (1705) in the records of the British generals that hinder us to fight and to improve our advantages as we might."

"August 7. This day there was a great preparation and all the appearances and dispositions for a battle. We were to attack the enemy (twenty battalions of us) through the wood of Soignies. The action threatened to be a bloody one, for they were well fortified, and occupied a strong post at Waterloo. . . . . . If it had come to a battle, in all probability it had been one of the bloodiest most of us ever saw. . . . There was also a stratagem to be used which, if it had taken effect, would probably have decided the battle in our favour. There were 20 battalions (ours was one) and horse conform, that were to march through a wood and post themselves quietly in the wood till we should hear that the battle was fully joined. Then we were to come out and attack them in the rear. Accordingly we marched at three in the morning and posted ourselves in the wood, where we stayed till three afternoon. General Churchill commanded us; but, the Duke finding it impossible to attack them, as I said, we came off."

"August 20. We have been these six weeks marching and countermarching, and seeking all occasions of coming at the enemy, yet our prospects have been blasted, and we have been kept as a lion in chains and cannot get out. There seems also to be a spirit of division sown among our generals, and as long as it continues I never expect we shall do any great things. I confess I begin to turn more dull than when the prospects of danger and death were more frequent."

army. But those who gave instructions for the inscription on his tombstone, designed him by the rank by which they were accustomed to know him ; and the following letter from the Duke of Marlborough to M. Hibelez, reads somewhat strangely in the light of a promotion received for services in the field.

"*Au Camp de Calmpt-hout, le 24 Octobre, 1705.*
"*Monsieur,*

"*J' ai été bien affligé, je vous assure, de la triste nouvelle que vous venez me mander de la mort de M. Ferguson. C' était un officier de mérite pour lequel j' avais beaucoup d' estime, et que je ne puis assez regretter : le public y a une grande perte, aussi bien que sa famille. Il est vrai que je faisais état d'abord que je serais arrivé en Angleterre, de prier la Reine de le faire général-major, et je ne doute point que S. M. y aurait consenti. Vous pouvez aussi faire fond que partout où il dependra de moi, je tâcherai de faire voir le cas que je fais de sa mémoire. Je vous prie d'en assurer Madame Ferguson et de me croire très-parfaitement.*
"*Monsieur, votre, &c., M.*"

His name, however, occurs once again in the despatches, for replying on 28th January, 1706, to letters of the Earl of Galway who then commanded the British forces in the Peninsula, the Duke wrote—" By the former you desire Mr. Ferguson might be spared to supply the place of Major-General in Portugal, but he had been dead near two months before the date of your letter."

"This day," says Blackader, writing in his diary two days after the former entry, "we were employed in the funeral of our Brigadier ;" and a few old accounts connected with the last scene have a certain melancholy interest, as showing how the obsequies of a general officer were conducted in those days in the Dutch garrisons. Eighty-four officers were provided with black scarves and gloves, twelve sergeants with crape, scarves, ribands, and gloves, and twenty-one ells of black cloth were obtained to cover twenty-one drums. There is an item for crape to cover Captain Ferguson's hat ; so much for "24 ells of crape for ye four colours, six ells to each ;" so much "for flambows and the men that bear them ;" so much "more to the twelve sergeants that bore his corps to the grave ;" so much "more for a sergeant and eighteen men who was the guard of his corps until his interment ;" and a sum "payed to Bertram where the officers met with Captain Lawson."

The town of Bois-le-Duc rises out of a broad plain, which, in winter, becomes an extensive marsh, and with its imposing ramparts, bastions, and moat (as yet almost untouched), still recalls the days of the Grand Alliance, when it formed winter quarters and base of operations for the hosts of Marlborough. Above the ramparts cluster the red tiled roofs, and above them again is seen the pile of the beautiful cathedral of St. John, situated in the highest part of the town. The floor of the cathedral, perhaps the finest in the Dutch dominions, is covered with tombstones bearing the escutcheons of the *noblesse* of North Brabant, but in the choir is a simple slab showing these inscriptions.*

---

* M. Hezenmans "l' archiviste de Bois-le-Duc" has been good enough to furnish the following note on these abbreviations. "Pierre tombale dans la cathedrale St. Jean à Bois-le-Duc (Hollande.) Coté sud-est du choeur. La seconde partie de l' inscription se lit : De Hoog Edel Gestrenge Heer, &c." These words were the Dutch style of an officer of rank, and would be translated literally as "the high, noble, and powerful seigneur," or perhaps more accurately, as "the right honourable and gallant gentleman."

Curiously enough, in formal documents the date of General Ferguson's death has been variously given. That on the stone agrees with the Duke of Marlborough's letter, and perhaps, also, allowing for the difference of style with the date given in a paper headed "Brigr. ffergusone his abstract ending 11th October, 1705, he died," and also with Blackader's entry, which is dated the 13th. But, the Inventory prefixed to a formal copy of his will, bears to be of the goods belonging to "Umq^{ll} Brigadier ffergusone, of Bomekellie, the time of his deceise, who deceised at the Bosch, in Braband, the 14th day of October, 1705 years, faithfully made and given up be himselfe at Mastrich, the 12th day of May, 1704 years."

My first knowledge of the stone described above was obtained on a visit to Bois-le-Duc in 1887 ; and a more careful examination of old accounts on returning to Scotland, disclosed one in Dutch which contained entries of "2 uuren luyden der klocken in de groote kerk," and "Het graft in 't choor."

One or two entries in the abstract corroborate Blackader's statement.

	Gilders.	
"16th October.—To ye Brigadier's Landslady and his fraught, from the Hague to Rotterdam, . . .	13	17
To Mr. Verdure at ye Hague, p. discharge given the Brigadier there, ...	173	0
17th.—for Lomond's at Rotterdam, Coach hier and passage money from Rotterdam to Gorkom, and for two botles of Bruntt Claret—in all, ...	10	0

D. O. M. S.
D. ABR. HIBELET.
ECCLESIÆ GALLO-BELG
PASTOR.
OBIIT 2 MAII.
MDCCXX.

DE H. ED. GESTR. HEER
IAMES FERGUSON.
BRIGAD.-GENERAL, &c.
OBIIT XXII OCT.
MDCCV.

The scene underneath the lofty arches of St. Jan's Kerk must have been an impressive one, on the October morning when the sergeant and 18 men moved up from the citadel beside the harbour with their charge, while the officers clustered round with their black scarves, and the colours and the drums were seen draped in black. Captain Lawson who took charge of the interment, and was a tutor under the will, would be busy and active; Lieut.-Colonel Borthwick wondering if the command was to come to him, which ultimately was given out of the regiment, and Captain Blackader musing on "the vanity of human grandeur." And when next the Scottish soldiers marched from Bois-le-Duc, one well-known figure was missing at their head; his charger was ridden by Major-General Murray; and the infant * baptized a few days before, and the elder children far away in Britain were never to meet in the home on the banks of the North Esk.

* The daughter, who so early lost her father, passed her life in Holland, marrying in 1730, M. Gerard Vink, Advocate, of Bois-le-Duc, grandson of M. Nieupoort, Ambassador to England, and brother of the Comptroller-General of the Dutch Fortifications.

Madame Ferguson married again, her husband being Captain Hendrick Chombach.

In the " Naam Lijst en Wapen kaart der Leden van de Regering de Pensionarissen Griffiers en Secretarissen van 's Hertogen Bosch," a record of all those who have held honourable office in Bois le-Duc, since its conquest by the Dutch, occur the names and arms of M. Johan Hibelet, Madame Ferguson's brother, who married a grand-daughter of the famous Admiral Tromp, of M. Bastide, her brother-in-law, of M. Chombach, one of her sons by her second marriage. and of M. Vink, a relative of her son-in-law. Her other son (Chombach) entered the Dutch army.

General Ferguson was succeeded in the command of the Cameronians by the Earl of Stair, who, on 13th January, 1706, granted a discharge to his children and executors, for "any sums laid out by me for arms and accoutrements for the use of the deceased Major-General Ferguson's Regiment, to whom I succeeded." Blackader's diary has told us the sensation of his comrades-in-arms on hearing of his death; Luttrell's preserves the ideas of the public. "Sat., Oct. 20, 1705. Yesterday we had three Dutch posts which advise . . . that Major-General Ferguson is dead in Holland, and much lamented, being an officer of great experience."

Such is the story to which the old commissions led us, of the career of one who worked his way like a true Aberdeenshire Scot, and did his duty well in spheres continuously enlarging. As soldier of fortune, in civil strife, and in a more satisfactory position in the armies of his country abroad, he manifested the same qualities—if not so distinguished, at least happier in their final direction—which in his countrymen, Gordon of Auchleuchries and Keith of Inverugie, were so valuable to Peter the Great and Frederick of Prussia. He had been fortunate in his opportunities, for he seems to have been present at nearly every action of magnitude in which the British troops were engaged during his life-time, except the Battle of the Boyne. The fell carnage of Killiecrankie had made him a major, the strewn fields of Steinkirk and Landen gave the remaining steps of regimental rank. The study of biography as subordinate and ancillary to history, affording side-lights and filling up the background, is calculated to correct an erroneous impression apt to be produced when we confine ourselves to accompanying the formal and dignified march of the national narrative. For there is a tendency to lose sight of the connection in the chain of events, and to consider different reigns and epochs, as if they were rather successive plays put upon the stage, than the development in various acts of one great drama. Nor is this tendency counteracted by the lives of those who performed the principal parts, and whose careers were crowded with events, for then we seem to be reading annals rather than memoirs, and time is forgotten in following action. But, as in ordinary life some small circumstance sometimes calls up the past in its relation to the present, so for those who care to note it, and amuse themselves by reading between the lines of history, the reappearance of some personage unknown to fame, furnishes a standard with which to measure others, lets in a sudden light on a dry narrative, and points out better than the moralizing it suggests, how events grew out of each other which on the page of history seem very far apart. Killiecrankie and Blenheim are names which call up a totally different set of associations, yet the story we have been tracing shows that from one point of view they were only separated by the distance between major and general. Borthwick, the major of the Cameronians in the campaign of 1704, had been wounded in the fierce fight at Dunkeld; and a Captain who was hit at Schellenberg, was again severely wounded in the action at Preston in Lancashire, which quelled the first Jacobite insurrection. The father of Brigadier Ferguson had mustered under the banner of Lord Huntly in the Scottish "Troubles"; one grand-nephew was narrowly to miss capturing Prince Charles and Flora Macdonald after Culloden; while another received "a very high compliment" from Admiral Rodney for his conduct in the naval action off Guadaloupe in 1780, and the fall of a great-grand nephew at King's Mountain in the same year marked the turn of the tide in the contest for the Southern Colonies which governed the issue of the American Revolution. Eighty-five years later the hoisting of the Federal flag on the Capitol of Richmond by a great-grand nephew of the American Loyalist officer, to whom fell the melancholy duty of surrendering on that occasion, signalized the preservation of a Union more fortunate in that respect, than the wider one of the preceding century. The search for such coincidences perhaps deserves no better designation than mere historical gossip; and to pursue it further would be to transgress the limits prescribed when we resolved to trace this story of a soldier of the Protestant succession. His experience in its main features is probably an illustration of that of many others—comrades and contemporaries; but there is one peculiarity in it that arrests the attention, for who that knows the real Scotland of the 17th century would expect to find the Cameronians within four years of the day they were embodied receiving a Colonel from Aberdeenshire? The Duke of Wellington once observed that he could never make

due allowance for, or understand the public men of William III.
and Queen Anne's time till he had seen how the characters of the
statesmen of France deteriorated during their Revolutionary
period; and amid all the treachery, vacillation, and intrigue which
marked even the Conservative Revolution, worked out under the
motto, "*Je maintiendrai,*" we turn with a sense of relief from the
politicians, who betrayed the master whose bread they ate, to the
straightforward soldiers who were true to their salt, and who, either
as officers of King James bearing the pains and penury of exile
without a murmur, or as steadfast supporters of William of Orange,
in whose early battles they had won their spurs, maintained alike
under the shadow of the Pyrenees, in the swift current of the
Rhine, or on the banks of the Meuse and the Moselle, the truth
of the old Continental proverb, *fier comme un Ecossais.*

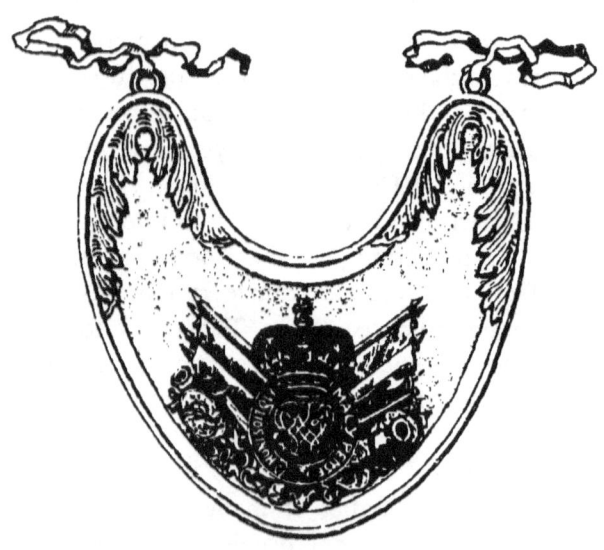

BRIGADIER FERGUSON'S GORGET.

II.

LIEUT.-COLONEL PATRICK FERGUSON,

A Soldier of the American Revolution.

"*The length of our lives is not at our own command, however much the manner of them may be. If our Creator enable us to act the part of men of honour, and to conduct ourselves with spirit, probity, and humanity, the change to another world, whether now or fifty years hence, will not be for the worse.*"—LETTER OF COLONEL P. FERGUSON.

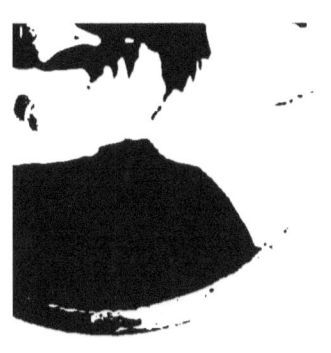

A SOLDIER OF THE AMERICAN REVOLUTION.

I.

THE FIRST BREECHLOADER.

"His was a full soul indeed, and that had every way a beautiful aspect: a soul of the old stamp and that had produced great effects had fortune been so pleased."—*Montaigne.*

"Ferguson was the friend of every man's merit, and had no enemy to his own."—*Dr. Adam Ferguson.*

"HAD Cleopatra's nose been but a trifle shorter, how different might have been the destiny of the world," is a well-known remark of Pascal's; and at least one incident in the experience of the young soldier whose name heads these pages, might afford food for somewhat similar reflections. The sword that menaced Damocles hung on a hair, and on the fate of persons comparatively unknown to fame the destinies of nations have sometimes seemed to turn. The story of the struggle that in last century rent their empire in twain, is one on which Britons naturally do not care to dwell; and he who recounts it on this side of the Atlantic, is justly liable to a similar protest to that which the appearance of Marmion drew from the patriotic lips of Leyden.

> "Alas, that Scottish maid should sing
> The combat where her lover fell;
> That Scottish bard should wake the string
> The triumph of our foes to tell."

Yet, in spite of the bitter memories, in spite of the errors of statesmen and the shortcomings of generals, while there is much to be learnt from the sore and painful experience, the conflict and its issue may be regarded without shame. In no war was more conspicuous gallantry displayed by British officers and soldiers, and the concession at the close was made after a heroic and honourable struggle against the combined forces of America and France, and Spain, and Holland. If the strife had been rashly begun, it was only continued after honest and generous efforts at reconciliation; and, as Lord Chatham recognised, had changed from aggression on Colonial independence to defence of Imperial unity. If in the long run we were defeated, it was by men of our own blood; and if we cannot but regret "the woefullest division" that "set this house against this house," we rejoice that our kinsmen have proved themselves so worthy, and used so splendidly the position which they bravely won.

If we cannot look without a sharp and bitter pang upon the sufferings of the American loyalists, which the cessation of warfare intensified, yet the pacification which involved catastrophe to them was only acccepted when it was clearly inevitable, and some sacrifice was made to secure them some compensation. And now that the hatchet has long been buried, when the statesmen of the United States are confronted by the same difficulties as trouble the old monarchies, and since the American people have poured forth their blood like water to maintain their Union; we are confident that on "the other side" the most active patriotism may coexist with honourable respect for the sentiments that refused to sacrifice without a struggle to the last, the brightest jewels of the British Crown, and with a chivalrous regard for the reputation of individual "foemen worthy of their steel."

Be these things as they may, the history of the American Revolution is fruitful in incidents where the ultimate issue seemed to tremble in the balance. The chances of the campaign that ended at Saratoga, the circumstances connected with the sad fate of André, and the mischances that, for a very brief period, gave the French fleet the command of the sea when "the great and good Cornwallis" was in sore straits at Yorktown, were all occasions when a very little would have changed the current of events. But passing these, where would American independence have been if during the dreary winter of the camp at Valley Forge, the quailing courage of Congress, and the flagging hopes of the half-clad "Continentals" had not been sustained by the high and steadfast spirit of the Virginian gentleman, which drew from Lord Stanhope the generous expression of lofty admiration—" surely we see displayed the hero's mind : calmly foreseeing defeat as certain, yet as calmly resolved to abide it in the path of duty, and to contest it as long as possible?" Yet how narrow an escape had Washington not very long before! And apart from the interest which the record of a brave man's life must always possess, the career which we now propose to trace deserves enquiry, because the battle in which Colonel Ferguson fell, and which was decided by his death, though insignificant if measured only by the numbers engaged, has been declared by careful students to mark the turning point of the second phase of the Revolutionary war, that was fought out in the the Southern States. As a mere personal biography the story has its charm, for it gives a picture of the stirring life which might be led by a younger son of a Scottish family in the eighteenth century, and shows that in what we are sometimes accustomed superficially to consider as the artificial age and jaded generation, on which there shortly burst the deluge of the French Revolution, it was possible to illustrate the truth so well expressed by Lord Beaconsfield, that "to believe in the heroic makes heroes."

Patrick Ferguson was born in 1744, and was the second son of an Aberdeenshire laird, James Ferguson of Pitfour, and Anne Murray, a daughter of the fourth Lord Elibank. His elder brother became in after years an attached supporter and personal friend of the younger Pitt, and represented his native county in Parliament for thirty years, comprising the period of the Revolutionary and Napoleonic wars. Their father had followed the legal profession, and after acting as counsel for the Jacobites at Carlisle in 1745, where an honourable stratagem is said to have saved the lives of not a few of his clients, and enjoying for sometime the blue riband of the Scottish bar as Dean of the Faculty of Advocates, was in 1764 raised to the bench as Lord Pitfour. An interesting biographical sketch of Colonel Patrick Ferguson was composed by Dr. Adam Ferguson, the eminent philosopher and historian of the Roman Republic, who, though not a kinsman—unless credence is to be given to an old and very vague tradition—was an intimate friend of his father's family, and probably also actuated by the Scottish sentiment of clanship. It was originally intended for the "Encyclopœdia Britannica," but the editor thought it too long, the author would not curtail it, and it was not inserted. A few copies were printed in 1817.

The little expedition in which Colonel Ferguson commanded in chief, and which was so disastrously terminated by his fall, while noticed as important in its bearings on a critical condition of affairs, is only referred to incidentally by British historians. But in the United States it has received that minute attention which the influence of the catastrophe that closed it, on the course of American history, deserves; and, commemorated in song and history, romance, tradition, and monumental stone, King's Mountain is regarded, in the language — emphatic, if somewhat mixed—of Jefferson, as "the joyful annunciation of that turn in the tide of success that terminated the Revolutionary War with the seal of our Independence." The brief campaign and the bloody battle have formed the subject of an elaborate monograph from the pen of the historian, Lyman C. Draper; while in article and lecture, General de Peyster has broken a lance in the cause of the denounced loyalists, and in defence of the fair fame of their gallant leader. For in the warmth of a patriotism that easily swells into rancour, and magnified by local traditions and impetuous annalists, apt to develop the fabulous, Ferguson and his "Tory" followers have often been credited with all the cruelty and vices never absent in civil wars, and which then, alas, were too often manifested by both sides in the peculiarly savage warfare which marked the Southern contest. But his contemporaries and closer and more careful scrutinizers of the past are at one in recognising in the British leader a soldier as humane as gallant, and as chivalrous as capable. It is gratifying to find that narrower research in hostile sources corroborates the high estimate formed by the opinion of his comrades, and recorded by his distinguished biographer. "It is usual and popular," writes General de Peyster, in New York, " to attribute the general irritation against Ferguson to his own severity and the outrages committed by his followers. This is totally inconsistent with the language used about him by local historians. It is needless to dwell on his intrepidity, for that he was utterly fearless is acknowledged by every one—likewise his extraordinary ability. If any one to whom he was nearest and dearest desires to hear his praises set forth in the strongest language they need only resort to Ramsey and Wheeler." Even the zealous patriotism of Draper, while occasionally betraying him into a rash expression, and inducing an incapacity to appreciate the position and principles of the Tories whom he denounces, which is almost ludicrous, does not prevent him paying a dignified, generous, and honourable tribute to the virtues and the valour of the Royalist commander, whose last moments he describes with graphic power and minute detail.

But we anticipate. "Patrick Ferguson," says his Scottish biographer, "fortunately united in his own character, the calm judgment and exalted abilities of his father, with the vivacity and genius of his mother's family. Those who associate ferocity with the military character will hardly believe in what degree a person so fond of the military life was humane and compassionate to his enemies, as well as affectionate and generous in his friendships." An interesting glimpse into the influences which aided to form his character, is afforded by a letter printed by Sir Wm. Fraser in his work on the Earls of Cromarty. It was from a brother of his mother, Brigadier-General James Murray, who was known in later years as "Old Minorca," from his spirited defence of that island against the forces of France and Spain, and who at this time had just succeeded the gallant Wolfe in command of the army which had triumphed on the heights of Abraham. He dates from "Quebec, Oct. 11th, 1759," and after observing that he had too great a share in the battle to descend to particulars, says—"I left orders to send Petty Ferguson to the accademy at Wolich. I hope it was done. I mean to push him in my own profession. I am sure if I live I shall have it in my power; and if I die it will not be the worse for him that I had the care of him." The auspices were good, and the time—that *annus mirabilis* in which the imperial policy of Chatham was illustrated by victories and conquests in every quarter of the globe—was an inspiring one for a young soldier entering on his career.

The boy "having early chosen," as Dr. Adam Ferguson writes,

in the balanced periods of the eighteenth century, "the life of a soldier, was sent to finish his education at a military academy in London, where he acquired the elements of fortification, gunnery, and other arts subservient to his intended profession. Of these he afterwards pursued the study in real situations—in action as well as on paper; and was sagacious, original, and inventive in the application of expedients to actual service." He certainly proved himself in later life to be a scientific soldier as well as a brave officer; but one would scarcely think that he could have obtained much practical knowledge at this academy, as he was only fourteen years old when he received his first commission in the Royal North British Dragoons—more familiar to fame from their services on many a stricken field as the Scots Greys. With them he served through some of the German campaigns—joining them soon after the action on the plains of Minden. On June 30th, 1760, the Dragoons aided in driving the French cavalry from the field, and chased their infantry in disorder through Warburg and across the Rymmel river, the commander-in-chief declaring that they had performed "prodigies of valour." On 22nd August their "brilliant charge" decided a contest near Zierenberg, and next month they captured Zierenberg with two cannon and 300 prisoners. Two episodes in particular, in the early part of the young soldier's career, are recorded as illustrating a spirit "which was indeed habitual to him." The first occurred in Germany before he had completed his sixteenth year. He and another young officer (Sir John Mitchell) were out on horseback a few miles in front of the army, when they fell in with a party of the enemies' hussars who gave chase. In passing a ditch Ferguson dropped one of his pistols, "but thinking it improper for an officer to return to camp with the loss of any of his arms, he releaped the ditch in the face of the enemy, and recovered his pistol." They halted, astonished at his boldness, and thinking that some unseen support must be at hand, and he completed his retreat in safety and with honour. The second incident happened at Paris some years after. An officer in the French service "spoke reproachfully in his presence of the British nation. This insult he not only resented on the spot, but surprised his antagonist next morning with a visit before he was out of bed. "This is well young man," said the other; "I have paid such visits, seldom received them; but it is fair to tell you that I am reputed one of the best swordsmen in France" "That is not the question now," said Ferguson, "you are in my debt—let us find a fit place to settle our accounts." They accordingly went to the Boulevards together; Ferguson considering how he might deprive this swordsman of the advantage of his superior skill; and the other regarding with security and contempt so young an antagonist. As soon as they had drawn, Ferguson rushed within his adversary's point, seized the hilt of his sword, and, in the scuffle, was so fortunate as to get possession of it. "You are a brave fellow," said the other, "and I shall certainly do you justice wherever our affair is mentioned.""

As, however, has been the case with more than one military and naval hero, Ferguson had to struggle with the disadvantages of a delicate constitution, and he had scarcely finished his first campaign when he was disabled by sickness, and after being some time in hospital was sent home, when in a state to be removed. We are told that "the late Dr. Armstrong, author of the celebrated poem of the Art of preserving Health, &c., was then physician to the British forces in Germany, and formed upon that occasion the warmest friendship and affection for young Cornet Ferguson, which continued till his death." But the young Cornet did not take so serious a view of his condition, and was anything but resigned to the decree of his doctors. Writing to his friend, General Watson, he said—"I am now entirely recovered, and might serve the next campaign with ease, had not the fears of my parents prompted them to apply for an order for my joining the light troop; by which means I am deprived, for these many years to come, of the only chance of getting a little insight into my profession." But though not in the field he was by no means idle. "Being much at home, from the year 1762 to the year 1768, he entered warmly into the question which was then agitated, relating to the extension of the Militia Laws to Scotland. He saw no difficulty in combining the character of a soldier with that of a citizen, so far as was necessary for the defence of a country in which citizens enjoy such invaluable privileges; and some of the ablest and most intelligent publications, which appeared in the public prints of the time, were of his writing."

In 1768 a company was purchased for him in the 70th regiment, and he joined his detachment at Tobago—an island of which his younger brother, George, became governor—where "he was of great service in quelling very formidable insurrections of the negroes." But in the West Indies he suffered much from ill health, and, after a short visit to North America, returned to Britain in 1774.

Always on the outlook for opportunities of action, he regarded with attention the aspect of affairs ; and the outbreak of war with the revolted colonies found him intent on the invention of a new species of rifle, with which to counteract the superiority as marksmen of the American backwoodsmen. It is, indeed, strange that more than a century ago, a breechloading rifle which enabled those armed with it to seize every advantage of cover,—"to have," in the words of the philosopher biographer, "the cover of a parapet behind even a consolidated molehill, or the least inequality of the earth's surface"—should have been brought into use and then lost sight of almost altogether. American writers note that Ferguson's rifle was "used with effect by his corps," and the biographer of Washington says of its inventor :— "The British extolled him as superior to the American Indians in the use of the rifle—in short, as being the best marksman living." This praise was not confined to his own countrymen. "According to the testimony of eyewitnesses," says Draper, "he would check his horse, let the reins fall upon the animal's neck, draw a pistol from his holster, toss it aloft, catch it as it fell, aim and shoot the head off a bird on an adjoining fence."

The first exhibition of the new invention was made before Lord Townshend, then Master-General of the Ordnance, and is thus described in the Annual Register of 1st June, 1776. "Some experiments were tried at Woolwich before Lord Viscount Townshend, Lord Amherst, Generals Hervey and Desaguiliers, and a number of other officers, with a rifle gun upon a new construction by Captain Ferguson of the 70th Regiment, when that gentleman under the disadvantages of a heavy rain and a high wind performed the following four things, none of which had ever before been accomplished with any other small arms, 1st. He fired during four or five minutes at a target, at 200 yards distance, at the rate of four shots each minute. 2nd. He fired six shots in one minute. 3rd. He fired four times per minute, advancing at the same time at the rate of four miles in the hour. 4th. He poured a bottle of water into the pan and barrel of the piece when loaded, so as to wet every grain of the powder, and in less than half-a-minute fired with her as well as ever without extracting the ball. He also hit the bull's eye at 100 yards, lying with his back on the ground; and notwithstanding the unequalness of the wind and wetness of the weather, he only missed the target three times during the whole course of the experiments. The captain has since taken out a patent for the said improvements." The invention attracted a good deal of attention, and before long was exhibited before the King at Windsor, by some men of the Guards. But, in the presence of Royalty, the marksmen were shy, and shot wild. "They would not," said the Captain, "be so embarrassed in presence of your Majesty's enemies." He then took a rifle himself, and "of nine shots which he fired at the distance of 100 yards, put five balls into the bull's eye of the target, and four within as many inches of it. Three of these shots were fired as he lay on his back, the other six standing erect. Being asked how often he could load and fire in a minute, he said seven times; but added pleasantly that he could not undertake in that time to knock down above five of his Majesty's enemies."

The patent of the Ferguson rifle was dated 17th March, 1776.* Its main peculiarities were the loading at the breech by means of an ingenious contrivance, by which the trigger-guard, acting as a lever, dropped a perpendicular plug or fine threaded screw, from flush with the top of the barrel to flush with the bottom of the bore, thus opening access to the chamber, and the provision of an elevating sight, "never in the way, nor to be moved out of its place." Various delicate adjustments secured the satisfactory working of the mechanism even with hot firing, and the patent also covered several inventions applicable to all firearms, and particularly adapted to artillery, as well as a new method of rifling. "The public," it asserted "is furnished with an arm which unites expedition, safety, and facility in using with the greatest certainty in execution, the two great desiderata in gunnery never before united."

* It was reprinted in 1854.

General de Peyster * thus describes the weapon, having before him Ferguson's own rifle. "The length of the piece itself† is 50 inches, weight 7½ lbs. The bayonet is 25 inches in length, and 1½ inches wide, and is what is commonly called a sword-blade bayonet; flat, lithe, yet strong, of fine temper, and capable of receiving a razor edge, and when unfixed as serviceable as the best balanced cut-and-thrust sword. The sight at the breech is so arranged that, by elevating, it is equally adapted to ranges ranging from 100 to 500 yards. Its greatest curiosity is, namely, the arrangement for loading at the breech. The guard plate which protects the trigger is held in its position by a spring at the end nearest the butt. Released from this spring and thrown around by the front so as to make a complete revolution, a round plug descends from the barrel, leaving a cavity in the upper side of the barrel sufficient for the insertion of a ball or cartridge or loose charge. This plug, an accelerating screw, is furnished with twelve threads to the inch, thereby enabling it by the one revolution, to open or close the orifice; so that the rifle is thereby rendered capable of being discharged seven times a minute. This accelerating screw constitutes the breech of the piece, only instead of being horizontal, as is usually the case, it is vertical. Were there not twelve independent threads to this screw it would require several revolutions to close the orifice, whereas one suffices." ‡ As

* In "Scribner's Monthly Illustrated Magazine," for April, 1880.
† It was given by the inventor to General Watts de Peyster's grandfather, Captain Frederick de Peyster, his favourite officer. An elder brother, Captain Abraham de Peyster, was second in command of the loyalist force at King's Mountain. Young Frederick de Peyster was then on detached duty. On 3rd April, 1865, his great-grandson, Lieut. J. L. de Peyster hoisted the Federal flag on the capitol of Richmond, receiving a brevet-colonel's commission for his "gallant and meritorious conduct."
‡ In Osbaldiston's "Universal Sportsman, or Nobleman, Gentleman, and Farmer's Dictionary" (Dublin, 1792) in an article on "Shooting" it is stated :—"By far the most expeditious way of charging rifled pieces, however, is by means of an ingenious contrivance, which now generally goes under the name of *Ferguson's rifle barrel* from its being employed by Major Ferguson's corps of riflemen during the last American War. In these pieces there is an opening on the upper part of the barrel and close to the breech, which is large enough to admit the ball. This opening is filled by a rising screw which passes up from the lower side of the barrel, and has its thread cut with so little

the bore of the British rifle was large and lead was scarce in the Carolinas, the Americans destroyed all the rifles captured at King's Mountain.

The time had now come for its inventor to enter upon the scene of action where his greenest laurels were gathered, and where in course of time his life was to be laid down. He volunteered for service in America, and obtained special instructions to the Commander-in-chief to have a corps of Volunteers drafted from the various regiments, armed in his own way, and put under his command. There was thus opened to him the opportunity of independent action, so dear to every aspiring spirit, and particularly prized by the soldier who in ordinary circumstances, would see nothing before him for a long time to come but the dreary routine of regimental duty. "This commission," says his biographer, "was agreeable to him chiefly because it gave him a species of separate command, and left him to conduct a corps which was formed upon a principle different from that of the rest of the army. He gave a signal specimen of its services at the battle of Brandywine, when, being advanced in the front of the column commanded by General Knyphausen, and supported by the rangers under Colonel Wemyss, he scoured the ground so effectually that there was not a shot to annoy the column in its march." His practical genius and scientific study of the art of war led him to excel in the very branches of military skill on which most stress is laid nowadays in the changed conditions of modern warfare. But the Commander-in-chief, Sir William Howe, was jealous of the formation of the rifle corps having been ordered without previous consultation with himself, and took advantage of Ferguson's being wounded, to reduce it and return the rifles to store. His merit, however, was "acknowledged throughout the army, and fully

obliquity that, when screwed up close, a half turn sinks the top of it down to a level with the lower side of the caliber. The ball being put into the opening above, runs forward a little way; the powder is then pressed in so as to fill up the remainder of the cavity, and a half round turn brings the screw up again, cuts off any superfluous powder, and closes up the opening through which the ball and powder were put. The chamber where the charge is lodged is without rifles, and somewhat wider than the rest of the bore, so as to admit a ball that will not pass out of the barrel without taking on the figure of the rifles, and acquiring the rotary motion when discharged.'

stated in the reports of the day to the Commander-in-chief, by whose orders the following letter was written to him by the Adjutant-General.

"Headquarters, 12th September, 1777.

"Sir,

"The Commander-in-chief has received from Lieutenant-General Knyphausen the most honourable report of your gallant and spirited behaviour in the engagement of the 11th, on which his excellency has commanded me to express his acknowledgements to you, and to acquaint you, sir, that he shall, with great satisfaction, adopt any plan that can be effected to put you in a situation of remaining with the army under his command.

"For the present, he has thought proper to incorporate the rifle corps into the light companies of the respective regiments. I am very happy to be even the channel of so honourable a testimony of your spirited conduct, and of that of your late corps. And I am, sir, with perfect esteem and regard,

"Your most obedient, humble Servant,
"(Signed)   J. Paterson, Adjt.-Genl.

"Capt. Ferguson, commanding the Rifle Corps."

It was well known in the army that Sir Wm. Howe had no love for the rifle-corps, and even carried his jealousy so far as to take no notice, in his official letter to the Secretary of State, of the conduct of the riflemen and their commander, which he had publicly acknowledged at the time. When this became known, on the "London Gazette," containing Sir William's letter, arriving in America, Capt. Ferguson sent a copy of the letter of thanks he had received to the Secretary of State.

The step taken by the Commander-in-chief caused him much mortification, all the more as the advantages of his weapon had been vindicated by the small loss suffered by his men, compared with that of the rangers. The rangers had seventeen men killed, and the rifle corps, who could load and fire without exposing themselves, only two men wounded, of whom he himself was one. Shortly before he received his wound, while he lay with a detachment of his riflemen on the outskirts of a wood in front of Knyphausen's division, a remarkable incident took place which must be narrated in his own words:—

"We had not lain long," he says in a letter to a friend, "when a rebel officer, remarkable by a hussar dress, passed towards our army, within a hundred yards of my right flank, not perceiving us. He was followed by another dressed in dark green or blue, mounted on a bay horse, with a remarkably large cocked hat. I ordered three good shots to steal near to them and fire at them; but the idea disgusted me. I recalled the order. The hussar in returning made a circuit, but the other passed again within a hundred yards of us, upon which I advanced from the wood towards him. On my calling, he stopped; but, after looking at me, proceeded. I again drew his attention, and made signs to him to stop, but he slowly continued his way. As I was within that distance at which, in the quickest firing, 1 could have lodged half-a-dozen of balls in or about him before he was out of my reach—I had only to determine; but it was not pleasant to fire at the back of an unoffending individual, who was acquitting himself very coolly of his duty; so I let him alone. The day after I had been telling this story to some wounded officers who lay in the same room with me, when one of our surgeons, who had been dressing the wounded rebel officers, came in and told us they had been informing him, that General Washington was all the morning with the light troops, and only attended by a French officer in a hussar dress, he himself dressed and mounted in every point as above described. I am not sorry that I did not know at the time who it was. Farther this deponent sayeth not, as his bones were broke a few minutes after."

The episode is a most romantic one, and the legal phrase that concludes Captain Ferguson's description of it, is suggestive of old Edinburgh associations, and the conversation of the old judge who had died at Gilmerton just three months before. With how much might the chamber of his rifle have been charged? His own account of the incident is of course the best evidence of all, but it ought to be observed that on authority only second to his own, some doubt has been expressed as to whether the officer, whom his chivalry preserved, was really Washington. According to Draper, James Fenimore Cooper related in the "New York Mirror," of 16th April, 1831, on the authority of his father-in-law, Major John P. de Lancey, some interesting facts corroborating the main features of the story. De Lancey was second in command of

Ferguson's riflemen, and had seen Washington in Philadelphia the year before the outbreak of the war. At Brandywine, says Mr. Cooper, the riflemen "had crossed some open ground in which Ferguson was wounded in the arm, and had taken a position in the skirts of a thick wood. While Captain de Lancey was occupied in arranging a sling for Ferguson's wounded arm, it was reported that an American officer of rank, attended only by a mounted orderly, had ridden into the open ground, and was within point-blank rifle shot. Two or three of the best marksmen stepped forward, and asked leave to bring him down. Ferguson peremptorily refused; but he went to the wood, and, showing himself, menaced the American with several rifles, while he called to him and made signs to him to come in. The mounted officer saw his enemies, drew his reins, and sat looking at them attentively for a few moments. A sergeant now offered to hit the horse without injuring the rider, but Ferguson withheld his consent, affirming that it was Washington reconnoitring, and that he would not be the means of placing the life of so great a man in jeopardy by so unfair means. The horseman turned and rode slowly away. To his last moment Ferguson maintained that the officer whose life he had spared was Washington. I have often heard Captain de Lancey relate these circumstances, and though he never pretended to be sure of the person of the unknown horseman, it was his opinion, from some particulars of dress and stature, that it was the Count Pulaski. Though in error as to the person of the individual whom he spared, the merit of Major Ferguson is not at all diminished." The difference of the two accounts is a good illustration of how men's recollections of what has taken place in action differ in the course of a few years; but Ferguson's own account, written shortly after the occurrence, must be taken as conclusive of what actually happened. The wound he received was of such a nature that, with all the assistance Captain de Lancey could give, it must have disabled him at once, and De Lancey's testimony is that of a witness speaking from memory, transmitted at second-hand. The calm bearing of the American officer is what we should expect from Washington, and the deliberate courage with which he quietly moved away on realizing his danger, is natural in one who would have been so important a capture, and recalls the coolness of

Marlborough when in similar peril from the French. If, on the other hand, it was the Count Pulaski, Ferguson was soon to meet him in circumstances calculated to quell any chivalrous compunctions towards the Polish adventurer.

The wound he had received was so severe as to disable him from service for some months. The ball had shattered the elbow joint of his right arm, and at first it was doubtful whether amputation would not be necessary. Although the arm was saved he never recovered the use of the joint, but, " with a spirit peculiar to himself, so assiduously practised the use of the sword and of the pen with his left that he scarcely seemed to have incurred any change but a difference in his handwriting." His regiment being stationed at Halifax, in Nova Scotia, he was now " no more than a mere volunteer with the army," and it was only at the discretion of the Commander-in-chief that he could be employed at all. " But," says Dr. Adam Ferguson, " every one concurred in favouring his pretensions, and in doing justice to his merit ; and what is uncommon, he showed an ardour for distinction and eminence without exciting proportional envy. His brother officers ever mentioned him with esteem and kindness. One of them, who kept a journal of the war, observed that, though careless of his own life to a fault, he was ever attentive to the means of preserving those under his command.—He was the friend of every man's merit and had no enemy to his own."

In the autumn of 1778, having earlier in that year been present at the battle of Monmouth, he had command of the land portion of a combined naval and military force, which was despatched from New York to root out a nest of rebel privateers which preyed upon the trade of that city from Little Egg harbour in the Jerseys. His troops only amounted to 300 British soldiers and 100 loyalists, and as the armament sailing from Sandyhook on the 30th September was delayed by contrary winds until the 5th of October, the enemy managed to get away some of their larger vessels. The others were removed over the bar into shallow water, where they were burnt to the number of ten or twelve by Captain Collins of the *Zebra*, who crossed the bar with his small craft, while the troops destroyed the quarters and store houses on shore.

Meanwhile a deserter brought intelligence that Pulaski, the Polish adventurer, in the service of the Congress—"reported to be the same who had carried off the person of his Polish Majesty with many circumstances of audacity and cruelty"—lay up the country with three companies of foot, three troops of horse, and a detachment of artillery, and that he had neglected to occupy a narrow bridge over a gully or creek about a mile in his front. This news immediately decided Ferguson to attempt a surprise. He embarked about 250 of his detachment in boats, set off at eleven at night, and after rowing about ten miles, landed at four in the morning within a mile of the bridge he had resolved to seize. Leaving fifty men to hold it, he advanced rapidly, and surprised Pulaski before break of day. The enemy lost several officers, including a lieutenant-colonel, a captain, and an adjutant, and about 50 rank and file. The following despatches published in the "London Gazette" of 1st December, 1778, supply Ferguson's own account of what Admiral Gambier termed "a spirited service."

Extract of a letter from Sir Henry Clinton, Knight of the Bath, to Lord George Germaine, dated October 25, 1778.

"In my letter of the 8th inst. I mentioned that my move into Jersey was partly to favour an expedition sent to Egg harbour. I have now the honour to enclose copies of two reports made to me by Captain Ferguson of the 70th regiment, who commanded the troops employed upon that service, to which I beg leave to refer your Lordship for an account of its success under direction of that very active and zealous officer."

Report by Capt. Ferguson, of the 70th Regiment, to His Excellency Sir Henry Clinton, dated Little Egg Harbour, October 10th, 1778.

"Sir,—I have the honour to inform you, that the ships with the detachment ordered to this place, arrived off the bar on the evening of the 5th instant, when Captain Collins sent in the galleys, but the ships could not enter before the 7th.

"Three privateers of 6 or 8 guns, with an armed pilot boat, had escaped out of the harbour before our arrival, in consequence of advice received, on the 2nd, from Mr. Livingston, warning them of our destination.

"As it was from this evident that preparations had been making against us for several days, it was determined to allow no further time, but to push up with our gallies and small craft, with what soldiers could be crowded into them, without waiting for the coming in of the ships; accordingly, after a very difficult navigation of 20 miles inland, we came opposite to Chestnut Neck, where there were several vessels and about a dozen houses, stores for the reception of prize goods, and accommodation for their privateersmen.

"The rebels had there erected a work with embrasures for 6 guns, on a level with the water, to rake the channel; and another upon a commanding eminence, with a platform for guns en Barbette, in which, however, it afterwards appeared that they had not as yet placed artillery.

"The banks of the river below the works being swampy, rendered it necessary for the boats with the troops to pass within musket shot, in order to land beyond them; previous to which Captain Collins advanced with the gallies to cover our landing, and as he came very close to the banks, and the guns of the gallies were remarkably well pointed, the fire from the rebels was effectually stifled; and the detachment landing with ease, soon drove into the woods the skulking banditti that endeavoured to oppose it.

"The seamen were employed all that evening and the next day till noon, in destroying ten capital vessels; and the soldiers in demolishing the village, which was the resort of this nest of pirates. Had we arrived by surprise, we meant to have pushed forwards with celerity to the Forks within thirty-five miles of Philadelphia. But as the alarm had been spread through the country, and the militia there had been reinforced from Philadelphia by a detachment of foot, five field pieces, and a body of light horse, our small detachment could not pretend to twenty miles further into the country to reach the stores and small craft there; and the shallowness of the navigation rendered it impracticable for the gallies to co-operate with us; it was, therefore, determined to return without loss of time, and endeavour to employ onr force with effect elsewhere; but some of our vessels having run aground, notwithstanding the very great diligence and activity of Captain Collins and the gentlemen of the navy, an opportunity offered, without interrupting our progress, to make two descents on the north side of the river, to penetrate some miles into the country, destroy three saltworks, and raze to the ground the stores and settlements of a chairman of their committees, a captain of militia, and one or two other virulent rebels, who had shares in the prizes brought in here, and who had all been remarkably active in fomenting the rebellion, oppressing the people, and forcing them, against their inclination and better judgment, to assist in their crimes.

"At the same time be assured, Sir, no manner of Insult or Tyranny has been offered to the peaceable inhabitants, nor even to such as, without taking a Lead, have been made from the Tyranny or Influence of their Rulers, to forget their Allegiance.

"It is my Duty to inform you that the officers and men have cheerfully undergone much Fatigue, and everywhere shown a Disposition to encounter any Difficulties that might offer.

"I have the honour to be, with the greatest Respect, &c.

"(Signed)   Pat. Ferguson, Capt. 70th Regt.

"P.S.—One soldier of the 5th was wounded through the Leg at Chestnut Neck, ; but we have neither lost a Man by the enemy nor Desertion since we set out."

Captain Collins described Captain Ferguson and his detachment as "performing a very gallant and meritorious piece of service," and having "shown the utmost zeal and forwardness to co-operate in everything for the advancement and Benefit of His Majesty's Service."

Report of Captain Ferguson, of the 70th Regiment, to his Excellency Sir Henry Clinton, dated Little Egg harbour, October 15, 1778.

"Sir,—Since the letter which I had the honour of writing to you on the 10th instant, Captain Collins has received a letter from Admiral Gambier, signifying that the Admiral and you are both of opinion that it is not safe for us to remain here, as the army is withdrawn from the Jerseys, and ordering our immediate return; but as the wind still detained us, and we had information by a captain and six men of Polaski's legion, who had deserted to us, that Mr. Polaski had cantoned his corps, consisting of three companies of foot, three troops of horse, a detachment of artillery, and one brass field piece, within a mile of a bridge which appeared to me easy to seize, and from thence to cover our retreat, I prevailed upon Captain Collins to enter into my design and employ an idle day in an attempt that was to be made with safety, and with a probability of success. Accordingly, at eleven last night, 250 men were embarked, and, after rowing ten miles, landed at four this morning within a mile of the defile, which we happily secured, and leaving 50 men for its defence, pushed forward upon the infantry of this legion, cantoned in three different houses, who are almost entirely cut to pieces. We numbered among their dead about 50, and several officers, among whom we learn are a lieutenant-colonel, a captain, and an adjutant. It being a night attack little quarter could of course be given, so that there are only five prisoners. As a rebel Colonel Proctor was within two miles, with a corps of Artillery, 2 brass twelve-pounders 1 three-pounder, and the militia of the country, I thought it hazardous with 200 men, without artillery or support, to attempt anything farther, particularly after Admiral Gambier's letter. The rebels attempted to harass us in our retreat, but with great modesty, so that we returned at our leisure, and reimbarked in security.

"The Captain who has come over to us is a Frenchman named Bromville. He and the other deserters inform us that Mr. Polaski has in public orders lately directed no quarter to be given; and it was therefore with particular satisfaction that the detachment marched against a man capable of issuing an order so unworthy of a gentleman and a soldier. It is but justice to inform you, sir, that the officers and men, both British and Provincials, on this occasion behaved in a manner to do themselves honour.

"To the conduct and spirit of Captain Cox, Lieutenant Lyttleton, and Ensign Cotter of the 50th Regiment, and of Captain Peter Campbell of the 3rd Jersey Volunteers, this little enterprize owes much of its success, as well as to the arrangements of Captain Collins of the navy, and attention of Captain Christian who accompanied the expedition.

"I have the honour to be, &c.

"(Signed)   Pat. Ferguson, Capt. 70th Regt.

"P.S.—The despatch vessel not having got to sea last night, I am enabled to inform you that our yesterday's loss consists of two men of the 5th, and one of the Provincials missing, and two of the 5th slightly wounded: Ensign Campbell of the 2nd Jersey Volunteers has received a stab through the thigh.

"We had an opportunity of destroying part of the baggage and equipage of Polaski's legion by burning their quarters: but as the houses belonged to some inoffensive Quakers, who, I am afraid, may have sufficiently suffered already in the confusion of a night's scramble, I know, Sir, you will think with us, that the injury to be thereby done to the enemy would not have compensated for the sufferings of these innocent people."

Bancroft, the American historian, in treating of this expedition, declares that the British, "cumbering themselves with no prisoners, killed all they could," but takes no notice of the consideration shown by troops flushed with success for the votaries of the unpopular doctrine of peace at any price.*

* It is right to notice that Draper describes the information given by the deserters as false.

When Sir Henry Clinton advanced in the following spring to dislodge the enemy from the posts of Stoneypoint and Verplanks Neck, Captain Ferguson was detached with a special command before the army, and "became a busy actor in the operations that followed." Stoneypoint was more than once taken and retaken, and as it appeared that these vicissitudes in its fortunes were partly due to faulty construction of the works, Ferguson was entrusted with the duty of remedying these defects. Although this was a service which would more naturally have fallen to the lot of an engineer officer, the engineers, it is said, "do not seem to have taken umbrage at it." "That Ferguson," says his biographer, "who had by this time attained the rank of Major, might erect what works he thought proper, it was proposed that he should remain in the defence of the place. Flattered with this opportunity to execute what he had often been meditating, he proceeded to realize some of his favourite ideas; and while he looked for an attack with all the anxiety of a person who waits the result of an interesting experiment, he had the mortification to receive an order to evacuate Stoneypoint, and join the army at New York, now destined to carry the war into a different quarter of the continent. In a letter to a friend on that occasion, full of regret, he says: ' Never did a fond mother leave her favourite child with more regret than I did that place.' He had the consolation, however, of being promoted to the rank of Major, and the prospect of being employed with distinction in the operations that were then projected." Indeed, though his engineering activity was put a stop to, his energies were to find another, and perhaps even more congenial field for exercise.

II.
THE "BATTLE SUMMER" OF 1780.

"The Gordon has asked him whither he goes,
Wheresoever shall guide me, the soul of Montrose."
—*Sir Walter Scott.*

"Superior Military genius is but rare among the gifts of nature; and, of who are endowed with it, many are stopt short in the early stages of a profession of which they are forward to incur the dangers. Such as survive these dangers, and attain to eminent stations in the service of their country, are secure of their fame. For those who fall prematurely, it is but fair, as often as they can be distinguished, to affix to their memory the marks of honour they covet, and for which the votaries of profit will not surely contend with them. If the young man who is the subject of the present article had escaped the dangers to which he was so often exposed, it is probable that the annals of his country would have spoken more fully for him."—*Dr. Adam Ferguson.*

THE war was now about to enter on its second great phase. The reconciliation mission to which Dr. Adam Ferguson had acted as secretary had failed of its object, although the large and liberal terms then proposed, included an offer to admit representatives of the States to the Parliament of Great Britain, and "comprehended every privilege short of a total separation of interests." The revolted Colonists had cast themselves into the arms of France. The result was not only to stiffen up both contending parties, but to confirm in adherence to the Imperial cause, many who had sympathised to a large extent with the original claims of the insurgents. The Royal commanders, while receiving an amount of support in America itself, which has been but faintly realised in this country, had never availed themselves adequately of the reserve of strength afforded by the loyalist convictions of a large section of the Colonial population. Thus, although regiments had been raised which had performed gallant services in the field, the loyalist strength in the Northern States had been largely frittered away, and though more than one gallant effort had been made in the South, the endeavours of the loyalists had been disconnected, and not supported as they ought to have been by the forces at the disposal of the British commander. Now, however, the British chiefs were alive to the magnitude of the efforts required, and the word was *toto certandum est corpore regni*. Recruiting had recently been active in New York and the Jerseys, and it was known that, in the Southern States, the elements of loyalty were even more zealous and widespread. The hopes of the loyalists had been raised by the remarkable success that had attended Campbell's appearance with a small force of Highlanders in Georgia. It was decided to appeal frankly and earnestly to them, to offer them the support of the British army in defeating the regular forces of Congress, and to devote all energy to the re-establishment of the Royal authority in the districts where its supporters were strongest, as the most effective means of securing the ultimate recovery of the whole Continent.

South Carolina had therefore been resolved upon as the sphere of the principal operations of 1780, and a powerful army was despatched from New York by sea for the reduction of Charleston. A small force, under Major-General Paterson, was landed at Tybee in Georgia, with orders to penetrate into South Carolina, it being desired that his advance should receive the main attention of the enemy, while the rest of the army again put to sea, and appeared before the city which was the objective of their operations. Paterson's route lay through a very difficult country, and on his flanks moved Major Ferguson and Major Cochrane with the infantry of the British legion. Both are described by Washington Irving as "brave and enterprising officers," and both, alas, were destined to an early death, for Cochrane, who was a brother of the Earl of Dundonald, had his head taken off by a cannon ball, while standing beside Lord Cornwallis at Yorktown, after a gallant ride across country with despatches. Their duties now were to reconnoitre the districts round, clear them of enemies, and collect boats and waggons for the use of the main body. One incident of this advance indicates the secret of the influence the loyalist officer obtained over the hearts of those with whom fortune brought him into contact, and testifies to his courage and composure. He and Cochrane had taken different routes, when they heard that one

Macpherson was in command of a large body of rebels at his own plantation on the road to Charleston. Both determined to surprise the place; but Ferguson reached it first, found it evacuated, and took up his quarters there. In the night, Cochrane arrived and immediately attacked, while Ferguson's detachment prepared to repulse what they believed to be an attempt of the Americans to retake the post. "Ferguson—as usual at the head of his men—attempting to parry a bayonet with his sword, received a thrust in the only arm of which he had any use; but while he raised his voice to encourage his men, he was known to his friend, Major Cochrane, who immediately put a stop to the conflict. Ferguson called for the man who had wounded him, and, giving him a piece of money, commended his alacrity, saying—'We should have known our friends sooner from their mode of attack.'"

This wound in the climate of the Southern States for some time threatened him with the loss of his other arm. But he continued his march, riding between two orderlies, and often obliged, to have the command of his horse, to hold the reins in his teeth, and as soon as his wound took a more favourable turn, he again took the field with all his former activity. His comrades rejoiced at the narrow escape made by "a life," says Major Hanger, afterwards Lord Coleraine, "equally valuable to the whole army and to his friends." "It was melancholy enough," wrote a participant in the affair, "to see Colonel Ferguson disabled in both arms, but thank God he is now perfectly recovered again." Tarleton commends "the intrepidity and presence of mind of the leaders" as having prevented more fatal results in this affray, and Hanger repeats that "the whole army felt for the gallant Ferguson."

Ferguson's special command at this time consisted of a corps of 300 men called the American Volunteers, formed of Loyalists from New York and the Jerseys, "he having the choice of both officers and soldiers, and for this special service he had given to him the rank of Lieutenant-Colonel." His rank in the British army at the time was that of Major of the (old) 71st, or Frasers' Highlanders. A diary of the Campaign written by Lieutenant Anthony Allaire, an officer of the American Volunteers, who were sometimes known as "Ferguson's Sharpshooters," has been preserved, and it shows that, during the siege of Charleston, his conduct was marked by the usual energy and enterprise. On the 2nd of May, with only sixty men of the American Volunteers, he "marched down to Mount Pleasant, and stormed and took possession of a little redoubt located partly on the main, and partly on the bridge that leads to Fort Moultrie." When Allaire saw the work, he "felt more surprised than ever in his life, for twenty men like the American Volunteers would have defied all Washington's army." On the 7th Ferguson obtained permission to attack Fort Moultrie itself, but on riding forward with four dragoons to reconnoitre found it already in possession of the British, having been surrendered to Captain Hudson of the Navy.

But his chief services were on detached duty, covering the army engaged in the siege, and he was employed along with Colonel (afterwards Sir Banastre) Tarleton, in clearing the country of parties of the enemy who endeavoured to harass the operations. On one occasion, falling in with an American convoy, he took 200 horses, 40 waggons, all their baggage, spare arms, and accoutrements without the loss of a man. It was owing to their association at this time that Ferguson and Tarleton have frequently had their names coupled as the most dashing leaders of light troops and irregulars that the contest with the revolted colonies produced. Tarleton was unequalled as a wielder of cavalry, Ferguson unrivalled as a commander of riflemen : and by the rapidity of their movements and the valour of their attack they became a terror to the disaffected. It is said that for long the exploits of Tarleton furnished the negro nurses of the Carolinas with a name of terror as effective for quieting troublesome children as that of Richard Coeur-de-Lion was found to be by the Saracen women of the days of the Crusaders, or the Black Douglas's by English mothers of the Northern Marches.* But the resemblance between the two British partizans only extended to the bold conception, and its vigorous execution. Too often did Tarleton justify the

* The "Aberdeen Journal," of 22nd January, 1781, preserves another parallel of the same kind in the following extract :—" The name of Tarleton is almost as dreadful to the ears of the Americans as the name of Talbot was to the French in the time of Henry VI., which they so much dreaded that whenever he appeared, or was supposed to command. the enemy used to cry out, ' Talbot and the devil,' and fly as if Belzebub himself was at their heels."

severe, though gentle, rebuke of the chivalrous Cornwallis, "There spoke the sabre;" but friends and foes agree in attributing to his comrade chivalry towards the weak, and humanity to the vanquished. "Ferguson," observes Washington Irving, in the life of Washington, "was a fit associate for Tarleton in hardy scrambling partizan enterprize; equally intrepid and determined, but cooler, and more open to impulses of humanity."

The American generals had established a chain of posts to keep up the connection between the beleaguered city of Charleston, and the districts in which they were supreme, to enable them to communicate with the garrison, and to afford supplies and reinforcements. These the British commander determined to destroy, and the surprise of the strongest and most distant of them, that commanded by General Huger at Monk's Corner was entrusted to Tarleton and Ferguson. It was completely successful; large captures were made, and the rebel force put to the sword, made prisoners, or dispersed. In the course of the marauding some dragoons of Tarleton's British legion broke into a house and insulted some ladies residing there. The ladies were rescued and despatched in a carriage to a place of safety, and the dragoons were apprehended. "Major Ferguson," we are told, "was for putting the dragoons to instant death;" but Colonel Webster, a superior officer who had by this time arrived, did not think his powers went so far, and they were sent to head-quarters and flogged. "We gladly," says Washington Irving, "record one instance in which the atrocities which disgraced this invasion met with some degree of punishment, and we honour the rough soldier, Ferguson, for the fiat of "instant death" with which he would have requited the most infamous and dastardly outrage that brutalizes warfare."

After the surrender of Charleston, dispositions were made to consolidate and organise the recovered province, and Ferguson was chosen for a service for which he had peculiar qualifications, and which gave a curious practical illustration of the views he had expressed in early days on the militia question. Among the inhabitants of the Carolinas there were many loyalists or "Tories," for, in that State, large numbers of Scottish Highlanders had settled, and there, as in the Mohawk valley in the far North, the royal troops were certain of a friendly welcome from the Highland colonists. Argyllshire, Skye, and Ross and Sutherland in particular, had sent their surplus population in large numbers to the fertile lands of the Carolinas. Under widely different conditions, and in a far distant scene, Ferguson was now to exhibit some of those qualities which, more than a century before, had enabled the great Montrose to achieve such astonishing results, with materials previously neglected or regarded with contempt. Possibly it was with some consideration for the feelings of a large number of those to whom he was now to appeal, that he was appointed Major of the 71st, a regiment raised in the Northern Highlands, from which many of these colonists had come. It was now proposed that "the well affected should be armed in their own defence," and he was entrusted with the duty of marshalling the militia over a large extent of country. In the proclamations he issued, in his new character of administrator, he called upon the people of South Carolina to restore the civil government of their country, under the favourable conditions then offered by the King and Parliament of Great Britain. A numerous militia was soon enrolled, who followed him "with the utmost spirit and confidence"; they were allowed to name their own officers, with the reservation that, as they had also to act as civil magistrates, the authorities should be satisfied that the appointments were only given to fit and proper persons, who would not abuse their trust. "Ferguson," says Dr. Adam, "exercised his genius in devising a summary of the ordinary tactics for the use of this militia, and had them divided in every district into two classes,—one of the young men, the single and unmarried, who should be ready to join the king's troops, to repel any enemy that might infest the province; another, of the aged and heads of families, who should be ready to unite in defending their own townships, habitations, and farms. In his progress among them he soon gained on their confidence by the attention he paid to the interests of the well-affected, and by his humanity to the families of those who were in arms against him." Historians of all opinions, and observers on both sides in the struggle unite in testifying to the ability and zeal manifested by the new Inspector-General of militia in the service now assigned to him. "He possessed," says General de Peyster," many of the qualities which ennoble a soldier. He was temperate in his habits, magnanimous in his disposition, fearless in danger, and manly at all times. Such was the confidence reposed in him by Cornwallis that he conferred on him a brevet of Lieutenant-Colonel; constituted him a local or territorial Brigadier-General of militia; confided to him an independent command, and allowed him to select his own subordinates and troops." Even to indicate the movements that ensued in the course of the subsequent operations, would, says the same writer, be almost equivalent to writing a complete history of the campaign in South Carolina during the "Battle Summer" of 1780. "Colonel Ferguson possessed qualities peculiarly adapted to win the attachment of the marksmen of South Carolina. To a corps of originally 150, but soon reduced by disease and hardship to 100 picked men, Provincial regulars (*i.e.* seasoned volunteers from New York and neighbouring States), armed with his rifles, he soon succeeded in attaching about 1300 or more hardy natives, until, as he advanced, his command increased to 2000 men, besides a small squadron of horse." But as we shall see, it was a fluctuating body, and on much of it little reliance could be placed. Its leader was to feel, as more than one Scottish leader who had achieved great things with the valour of the Highland clans, had felt, how unreliable their devotion was for sustained effort and support at critical moments. Meanwhile his powers were not merely military, but in the absence of constitutional civil authority, extended to matters not often within the sphere of a soldier's duty. He was even authorised to perform the marriage service, a significant illustration of the disorganised state to which prolonged civil war had reduced the district; and Lord Cornwallis writing to Sir Henry Clinton, described "the home duty as being more that of a Justice of Peace than of a soldier." For these diverse trusts, in which the statesman's tact as well as the soldier's courage was necessary, "no one," says Draper, "could have been better qualified than the distinguished partisan selected for the purpose. He seemed almost a born commander. His large experience in war and partiality for military discipline, superadded to his personal magnetism over others, eminently fitted him for unlimited influence over his men and the common people within his region. He was not favoured, however, with a commanding personal presence. He was of middle stature, slender make, possessing a serious countenance; yet it was his peculiar characteristic to gain the affections of the men under his command. He would sit down for hours, and converse with the country people on the state of public affairs, and point out to them, from his view, the ruinous effects of the disloyalty of the ringleaders of the rebellion . . . . He was as indefatigable in training them to his way of thinking as he was in instructing them in military exercises. This condescension on his part was regarded as wonderful in a king's officer, and very naturally went far to secure the respect and obedience of all who came within the sphere of his almost magic influence." At the same time his energy in action and tenacity of purpose was such as to gain from his comrades the epithet of "Bull-dog Ferguson," while those who met him in battle and felt the vigour of the onset which he led, alluding to his disabled right arm, shattered at Brandywine, spread in the Carolinas an unfeigned respect for one, distinguished among the fierce inhabitants of these wild regions as "the one-armed devil."

"The precise point," remarks Lord Bolingbroke in a striking passage, "at which the scales of power turn, like that of the solstice in either tropic, is imperceptible to common observation; and in one case, as in the other, some progress must be made in the new direction before the change is perceived." But when, in after years, events are traced back to their causes, and the period of equilibrium between the opposing forces is narrowed by diligent investigation, the interest heightens as the crisis is approached. It is emphatically so in the case of the events we are about to trace, for competent judges have expressed the opinion, that on the success of the Southern campaign of 1780 depended the integrity of the British Empire. "We are come," says Bancroft, the American historian, in dealing with this phase of the great struggle, "to the series of events which closed the American contest, and restored peace to the world. In Europe the sovereigns of Prussia, of Austria, of Russia, were offering their mediation; the United Netherlands were struggling to preserve their neutrality; France was straining every nerve to cope with her rival in the four quarters of the globe; Spain was exhausting her resources for the conquest of Gibraltar; but the incidents which overthrew the ministry of North, and reconciled Great Britain to America, had their springs in South Carolina."

In the second week of September Lord Cornwallis commenced his march towards North Carolina, having detached Ferguson to the western confines of South Carolina. The latter had with him his own corps of Provincial riflemen, and a body of local royalist militia, his force being variously estimated at from 400 to 1200 men. He was to visit each district, and procure lists of the militia on the spot. "His orders were," says Washington Irving, "to skirr the mountain country between the Catawba and the Yadkin, harass the Whigs, inspirit the Tories, and embody the militia under the royal banner.* He had been chosen for this military tour as being calculated to gain friends by his conciliating disposition and manners; and his address to the people of the country was in that spirit: 'We come not to make war upon women and children, but to give them money and relieve their distresses.'" From other sources we learn that he added, "he hoped they would excuse him if, meeting with their husbands or brothers in the field, he should use them a little more roughly." "Ferguson, however," says the American author, "had a loyal hatred of Whigs, and to his standard flocked many rancorous Tories, besides outlaws and other desperadoes; so that, with all his conciliating intentions, his progress through the country was marked by many exasperating excesses."

Two or three characteristic incidents of personal interest have been preserved by American tradition. While in the region of Old Fort, it is said that a party which Ferguson personally commanded, halted at the house of Captain Lytle, a noted rebel partisan. Mrs. Lytle appeared at the door in her best attire, and when the Colonel rode up and enquired for her husband, invited him to come in. He thanked her, but said his business required haste; that the king's army had restored his authority in all the southern provinces, and that the rebellion was virtually quelled;

---

* "This resolute partisan"—"that doughty partisan officer'—*Washington Irving*. "The ablest British partisan"—"known for his services in New Jersey and greatly valued"—*Bancroft*. " Celebrated," " indefatigable," " redoubtable," are the epithets of other American writers.

that he had come up the valley to see Captains Lytle and Hempthill, and a few others who had served in the rebel army against the king, and that he was the bearer of pardons for each of them. On Mrs. Lytle replying that her husband was from home, he earnestly asked if she knew where he was. She said she only knew he was with others of his friends whom you call rebels. "Then," said Ferguson," I have discharged my duty : I felt anxious to save Captain Lytle, because I learn that he is both brave and honourable. If he persists in rebellion and comes to harm, his blood be upon his own head." On the lady replying that her husband would never desert his country, it is said the Colonel rejoined that he admired her much as the handsomest woman he had seen in North Carolina, that he even half-way admired her zeal in a bad cause ; "but," he added, "the rebellion has had its day, and is now virtually put down. Give my kind regards to Captain Lytle, and tell him to come in. He will not be asked to compromise his honour : his verbal pledge not again to take up arms against the king, is all that will be asked of him." He then bowed to Mrs. Lytle and led off his troop. Unfortunately for that good lady, a straggler in the rear, less chivalrous than his commander, rode back and carried off her bonnet as a prize for some friend at home. On another occasion an active Republican, called Hampton, was brought as a prisoner to Ferguson's headquarters. Some of his local enemies had declared before the prisoner, that "Ferguson would put so notorious a rebel to death the moment he laid eyes on him "; but on the security of a Loyalist officer, he was allowed to remain overnight at home, under a pledge to present himself next morning. When he appeared and had given his name, a Major Dunlop entered, who did not possess the humanity of his chief, and asked his name. Ferguson replied, "Hampton," and Dunlop asserted that he was brother to a rebel he had killed, and himself one of the worst in the country, and ought to be strung up at once. But Ferguson dismissed both Hampton and a companion on parole. Hampton observed that when he wrote the paroles he did so with his left hand. One other act, trivial in itself, but significant as an illustration, may be noticed. A soldier had killed a fowl belonging to a farmer's wife, and on discovering it, she "promptly reported the theft to Ferguson." The British commander had the culprit immediately punished, and gave the good woman a dollar in compensation for her loss.

His movements in the Carolinas on this service were interrupted by a visit to headquarters, after Lord Cornwallis's victory at Camden in August. Prior to that time he had moved on his left in the interior, "acting with vigour and success against different bodies of the rebels," and detaching parties to bring in recruits and provisions, and clear the country of the Republican partisans. He personally "swooped down like an eagle" upon a party which had obtained a success over detached royalists, and forced them to take to flight. In the "Diary of a Carolina Loyalist in the Revolutionary War," published from his father's manuscript,* by General F. R. Chesney, of Euphrates Valley fame, one or two incidents are recorded by an active participator. When encamped at Thicketty Creek, Ferguson, says Chesney, "requested me to carry an express to Captain Moore, then commandant of Anderson's Fort on the North Carolina side, with a private message to hold the fort till the last minute." Before Chesney returned the force had moved to Tiger river, where they heard that the fort had surrendered to the Americans under Colonel McDowell. "This," says Chesney, "disappointed Ferguson's scheme of bringing the Americans to battle while attacking it"; and among his papers at King's Mountain there was a letter, apparently intended for Cornwallis, giving a description of the strength of the post, and speaking in plain terms of the cowardice that had sacrificed it. Chesney was then selected to reconnoitre the rebel camp at Cherokee ford, which he successfully accomplished. "I found," he says, "a loyalist whom I could confide in, and sent him off with the particulars by one route to Colonel Ferguson, whilst I went by another; and the Colonel got intelligence in time to intercept the enemy at the Iron Works, and defeat them. In returning I was taken by a party of rebels, who took from me a rifle borrowed of my brother-in-law; but as soon as they set out for the rebel camp, I made my escape, joined Colonel Ferguson, and received his thanks and friendship. . . . On August 9th, I was appointed captain and assistant-adjutant-

* *Vide* "Modern Military Biographies."

general to the different battalions now under Colonel Ferguson. The same day we attacked the enemy at the Iron Works, and defeated them with little trouble to ourselves, and a good deal of loss to the Americans." "The Americans," says Draper, treating of this occasion, "were compelled to make a hasty retreat, leaving one or two of their wounded behind them; but they were treated by Ferguson with great humanity." "Our next route," says Chesney, "was down towards the Fishdam ford on Broad river, where there was a fight (August 12), near the mouth of Brown's Creek, with Neil's militia, where we made many prisoners." Then came a moment of doubt, when "the half-way men (as those not hearty in the cause were called) left us"; then the good news of Camden, and then another movement to meet the rebels under McDowell, who had been victorious at Musgrove's Mills on the Enoree, but were at once driven to the interior by Ferguson's rapid advance. The pursuit was hot, but the Americans made good their retreat.* On the 1st of September, Allaire noted in his diary, that while the Provincials lay at Culbertson's plantation, near Fair Forest river, "Major Ferguson joined us again from Camden with the disagreeable news that we were to be separated from the army, and act on the frontiers with the militia." Lord Cornwallis had now set out from Camden through the Waxhaws to Charlotte in North Carolina; on his left, Tarleton was detached with his cavalry and the light and legion infantry, to move up the banks of the Wateree, while Ferguson, with his small detachment of provincials and the militia, was to move parallel to both.

In pursuit of McDowell he advanced as far as Gilbert-town, where he encamped for four days, and there the news reached him which determined his fate. His mission, hitherto, had been most successful. Lord Cornwallis had, however, in reporting its auspicious progress to the Home Government, noticed one element of weakness. "In the district of Ninety-six," he wrote on 20th August, "by far the most populous and powerful of the province,

---

* "Major de Peyster, with a strong body of mounted troops from Ferguson's column, pursued closely until late in the evening of the second day after the action at Musgrove's Mills, and did not draw rein until excessive fatigue and the fearful heat of the season and region, broke down both men and horses."

Lieutenant-Colonel Balfour by his great attention and diligence, and by the active assistance of Major Ferguson, who was appointed Inspector-General of the Militia of this province by Sir Henry Clinton, had formed seven battalions of militia, consisting of above 4000 men, and entirely composed of persons well affected to the British Government, which were so regulated that they could with ease furnish 1500 at a short notice for the defence of the frontier or any other home service. But I must take this opportunity of observing that this militia can be of little use for distant military operations, as they will not stir without a horse; and on that account your Lordship will see the impossibility of keeping a number of them together without destroying the country." This last consideration was doubtless present to Ferguson's mind, though his own spirit led him not to share the foreboding which seems to have troubled Cornwallis from his letter of the 29th :— " Ferguson is to move into Tryon county with some militia, whom he says he can depend upon for doing their duty, and fighting well; but I am sorry to say his own experience, as well as that of every other officer, is totally against him." *

But no anticipation of disaster was felt by Ferguson till immediately before it came, for the storm gathered as suddenly as it burst fiercely. At present the aspect was serene. When he encamped at Gilbert-town, "for many miles around people wended their way to the head-quarters of this noted representative of the British Crown." Among them were a number of ladies. " After the affair at Cane Creek, and the final retirement beyond the mountains of embodied whig forces in the western region of the Carolinas, Ferguson thought the matter decided. When William

* On this Sir Henry Clinton's observation seems not unjust, who "could not help being of opinion that the loss of Colonel Ferguson was owing, in a great measure, to Lord Cornwallis having detached Colonel Ferguson with a body of militia without any support of regular troops, notwithstanding, his lordship had informed Sir Henry Clinton—although that brave and zealous officer, judging of himself, had hoped he could make the militia fight without any support of regular troops." As regards the sending of relief when the detachment was in jeopardy, Lord Cornwallis writes : " My not sending relief to Ferguson, although he was positively ordered to retire, was entirely owing to Tarleton himself; he pleaded weakness from the remains of a fever, and refused to make the attempt although I used the most earnest entreaties."

Green rode up with a troop of cavalry and tendered his and their services for the defence of the King's cause, Ferguson thanked them for their loyalty, but declined their acceptance as the country was subdued and everything quiet." Shortly before he had paroled a prisoner taken at one of the skirmishes on the Pacolet or Enoree, with a verbal message to the leaders of the bands from beyond the mountains, who had swelled the previous incursions, to the effect that, "if they did not desist from their opposition to the British arms, he would march his army over the mountains, hang their leaders, and lay their country waste with fire and sword."

He had at this time dismissed many of the militia on furlough, his provincials, by the time he reached King's Mountain, were reduced to 70 men, and they were the only troops approaching to regulars and armed with the bayonet, under his command. He had, however, made some of the local militia extemporise a substitute for the bayonet by whittling down their knife-handles, and inserting them in the muzzles of their rifles. On 24th September he received an express from Colonel Brown, who commanded the royal forces at Augusta, in Georgia, informing him that a body of rebels, under one Clarke, who had been repulsed in an attack on that fort, were retreating by the back settlements of Carolina. Brown added that he was going to hang on their rear, and if Ferguson would cut across their route, they might be intercepted and dispersed. "As this service was perfectly consistent with that in which he was employed, Ferguson gave way to his usual ardour, and pushed with his detachment, composed of a few regulars and militiamen, into Tryon County." He was more adventurous than his comrade, and meanwhile the clouds were gathering around him. We have seen that his force had encountered a party of Americans, under McDowell, at Cane Creek, near the Broad River, and, after defeating them, "pursued them to the foot of the mountains, and left them no chance of safety, but by fleeing beyond the Alleghanies." * They spread the account in those regions of

---

* "Colonel Ferguson," says Chesney, " soon after got intelligence that Col. McDale was encamped on Cane and Silver Creeks, on which we marched towards the enemy, crossed the winding creek 23 times, and found the rebel party strongly posted towards the head of it near the Blue Mountains. We

Ferguson's force, its distance from its supports, and the possibility of overwhelming it before succour could arrive. Numerous backwoodsmen and others were already in arms, with the intention of seizing on the presents for the Cherokees, which were understood to be but slightly guarded at Augusta. The leaders of the "western army," as those from beyond the mountains designated themselves, sent expresses to Campbell, who set out to meet them with 400 men from South-Western Virginia, and to Col. Cleveland in North Carolina. They were joined by various other parties, and formed a force formidable, not only in numbers, but in composition. For these fierce backwoodsmen were not men to whose hands arms were new, but had been trained from youth to the wildest partizan warfare in bloody conflict with the Indians. They were skilled in the use of their own weapon, the Deckard rifle, and the country in which they were about to act was one that favoured the woodfighting and cover-slaughter in which they were adepts. They had been "born and grown up in an atmosphere of danger." Well appointed for their work, moving rapidly, and ready at once to seize an advantage, they were in such a country, awkward antagonists for the best light troops, and an enemy terrible to raw militia. And, ignorant of the usages of civilized warfare, they were a bad foe to be defeated by. The word now passed round told them that their business was "to catch and destroy Ferguson," before he could be supported or escape.

On the 30th of September the news of the imminent invasion reached Ferguson. It had already made Brown and Cruger discontinue their pursuit of Clarke; and Ferguson, who had advanced much further with the same object, realised at once the gravity of the situation. He halted and commenced to fall back towards Cornwallis. Finding his numbers scanty, he at the same time endeavoured to increase them and collect the royalists for one final effort. "Threatened," says Washington Irving, "by a force so superior in numbers and fierce in hostility, he issued an address to rouse the tories." "The aspect," writes General de Peyster,

---

attacked them instantly, and after a determined resistance, defeated them, and made many prisoners. The rest fled towards Turkey Cove in order to cross the mountains, and get to Holstein."

" of the stormclouds, portending a veritable cyclone, gathered upon the neighbouring mountains was too indicative not to have an effect upon even such a fearless man as Ferguson. It seems to have demoralized the royalists of this section. His circular letter to overcome its effects and their timidity, of the 1st October, breathes an indignation and contempt, which alone could have induced an elegant gentleman to pen such a scathing appeal in the roughest Saxon to even tepid manhood." That letter is in these terms :—

"Denard's Ford, Broad River, Tryon County.
"October 1st, 1780.

"Gentlemen :—Unless you wish to be eat up by an inundation of barbarians who have begun by murdering an unarmed son before the aged father, and afterwards lopped off his arms, and who, by their shocking cruelties and irregularities, give the best proof of their cowardice and want of discipline :—I say, if you wish to be pinioned, robbed, and murdered, and see your wives and daughters, in four days abused by the dregs of mankind—in short, if you wish or deserve to live and bear the name of men, grasp your arms in a moment and run to camp.

"The Backwater men have crossed the mountains : McDowell, Hampton, Shelby and Cleveland are at their head : so that you know what you have to depend upon. If you choose to be degraded for ever and ever by a set of mongrels, say so at once, and let your women turn their backs upon you, and look out for real men to protect them.

"Pat. Ferguson, Major 71st Regiment."

His first intelligence had been received from two deserters : it was soon corroborated, and, though he at once determined what course to pursue, that course has been the subject of much surprise and questioning. He sent more than one despatch to Lord Cornwallis asking for reinforcement. One of these, undated, but believed to have been written on the 6th of October, was in these terms :—

"My Lord :—A doubt does not remain with regard to the intelligence I sent your Lordship. They are since joined by Clarke and Sumter,—of course are become an object of some consequence. Happily their leaders are obliged to feed their followers with such hopes, and so to flatter them with accounts of our weakness and fear, that if necessary I should hope for success against them myself: but numbers compared that must be but doubtful.

"I am on my march towards you by a road leading from Cherokee Ford north of King's Mountain. Three or four hundred good soldiers, part dragoons, would finish the business. *Something must be done soon.* This is their last push in this quarter, &c.

"Patrick Ferguson.'

Dr. Adam Ferguson gives another version of the communication with headquarters, which seems to be based on another and apparently a later despatch. "He despatched a messenger to Lord Cornwallis, to inform his Lordship of what had passed—of the enemies he had to deal with, and of the route he had taken to avoid them; earnestly expressing his wish that he might be enabled to cover a country in which there were so many well-affected inhabitants: adding that for this purpose he should halt at King's Mountain, hoping that he might there be supported by a detachment from his Lordship, and saved the necessity of any further retreat. This letter, having been intercepted, gave notice to the enemy of the place where Ferguson was to be found; and though a duplicate sent on the following day was received by Lord Cornwallis it came too late to prevent the disaster which followed." One messenger was intercepted, and the other delayed. By Ferguson's orders Chesney "sent expresses to the militia officers to join" the detachment at King's Mountain, but the attack was delivered before any support arrived.

It is generally asserted that had Ferguson fallen back directly on receipt of the first intelligence, he could have reached Cornwallis, at Charlotte, in safety. As a matter of fact he made "an eccentric retreat." "There are only two explanations," writes General de Peyster, a practised critic of strategical movements, "for Ferguson's movements. Either he expected to be reinforced by Tory organisations, or he did not know the extent of the force about to overwhelm him. The latter alternative contradicts received opinions, and is the best proof that he acted in accordance with a plan which he considered judicious—a plan which he carried into the grave with him." His action, however, seems susceptible of easy explanation in the light of Dr. Ferguson's account. Personally, he had implicit confidence in the fighting qualities of the men he had raised; and those who were with him did stand by him bravely, for an hour of desperate fighting of the kind that is most demoralising even to seasoned troops. "He was not afraid of the mountain-men" on anything like equal terms, and there was much to make the facing them "necessary" to a man of his chivalrous character. His objects were twofold: to gain time till he should be reinforced by Cornwallis, or by the militia on furlough who had so recently flocked to the royal standard; and to cover the loyal province and maintain the results already accomplished. For immediate retreat beyond a certain point meant their absolute surrender to an incursion of barbarians: the uprising of all the disaffected, and the return of anarchy. To Ferguson personally these objects were very dear, and in the interests of the country the time was one most critical. He must have felt, in the words of Don John of Austria, that "our lives are staked upon this game"; and on considerations of sober policy, although the stakes were high and the forfeits immense, yet it was a game well worth the playing. Realizing the danger and the difficulty, he also recognised his prospects and saw his duty. And in that view his course was marked by foresight and ability. Resolved to "stand the hazard of the die," and conscious of its peril, he omitted nothing that could conduce to success. A skilful detour threw the enemy off the scent, as he fell back to a position of apparent strength and commanding situation; expresses were sent out in every direction to rouse the loyal, and every effort made to secure aid from Cornwallis. But a lucky capture informed the non-plussed Americans of his movements, the misfortunes of his messengers frustrated the hope of relief from headquarters, and the militia failed to respond in time. "Like any wise commander," says de Peyster, "he fell back on his supports, and they proved the veriest Pharaoh's reeds." A body of 600 men indeed, under Major Gibbs, were assembled four miles from the Americans at Cowpens, and on the morning of the 7th were only fifteen or twenty miles from Ferguson. Had they joined him, as it was expected they would in the course of the day, or had they marched to the firing, and fallen on the Americans while still held in check by the gallantry of the Provincials, the battle would undoubtedly have had a different ending. By so little did his last resource miscarry! "The haughty Scotsman," observes Draper, "relied this time too much on the pluck and luck which had hitherto attended him. In his own expressive language, a direful 'inundation' was impending."

III.

KING'S MOUNTAIN.

>   "On Tuesday last,
> A falcon, towering in his pride of place,
> Was by a mousing owl hawked at and killed."
> —*Shakespeare.*

>   "To such as he, oh! terrible
>   Dark rider through the world,
>   Thou com'st not ill upon the wings
>   Of the rushing battle whirled.
>   "In such as he the flame that glows
>   Through life to high renown,
>   Is better blown out suddenly,
>   Than slowly flickering down
>   "Through leaden days to nothingness;
>   Fitter for all such ones
>   Their lofty souls should march away
>   To the music of the guns."
> —*Hamilton Aidé.*

It was on the evening of Friday, the 6th of October, that Ferguson took post on King's Mountain. It had frequently been his practice to encamp on or near some great landmark. For three weeks he had kept his quarters on a hill, eleven miles south of Cedar spring, and two south of Glenn's spring, earlier in the year; for some time he had camped in close proximity to a "lofty peak, known in all that region as Pilot Mountain, almost isolated in the midst of a comparatively level country," and an eminence near Gilberton was known as Ferguson's Hill. He now fixed on King's Mountain as a commanding position in which to await the expected aid, and, if necessary, make a stand and fight it out to the last. "The situation of King's Mountain," said one of his loyalist followers, "was so pleasing that he concluded to take post there, stoutly affirming that he would be able to destroy or capture any force the whigs could bring against him." With the faculty of inspiriting his followers by happy allusion to fortuitous circumstances, which is part of the genius of a born commander, he observed that "this was Kings Mountain and he was king of the mountain." It is said that he added with a touch of profanity—more redolent of the region than consonant with his character—that "the Almighty could not drive him from it."*

Meanwhile the mountainers were anxious for their prey. At Cowpens, on Broad river, the western army had been joined by Williams, another American leader who, with 450 horsemen, had been acting against Ferguson. The combined force has been described by an officer who served in the war, as "a swarm of backwoodsmen, the wild and fierce inhabitants of Kentucky, and other settlements westward of the mountains, under the Colonels Campbell and Boon, with these of Helston, Powell's Valley, Barclay, Bottetourt, Augusta, and Fincastle, under the Colonels Cleveland, Shelby, Sevier, Williams, Brand, and Lacy." But American writers say that the British were misled by the resemblance of Nolachucky to Kentucky, and that the traditions of "the dark and bloody ground" do not embrace any share in the deeds of King's Mountain. About the 2nd of October, two whig scouts, who hung on the rear of the British, captured a British soldier who had loitered behind the rest, as he hastened to regain the column. "The redcoat proved to be Ferguson's cook, and it seems was completing the preparation of a savoury meal to take along for the Colonel's breakfast, who had been too busy in getting his troops started to enjoy his morning's repast." After learning from him the movements of the British, they let the cook go, but kept the breakfast. The man was dismissed with a note to Ferguson, in which the captors announced that they had sent him back on learning his important position. On reaching the camp he delivered the note, telling his experiences, and cursing his captors in unmeasured terms. "Ferguson quietly restrained his temper, and told him he was wrong to speak of them so harshly, as they

---

* The American writers report the energetic expression in different terms, and it is inconsistent with the serious though resolute tone of the despatch to Lord Cornwallis.

had used him well, and permitted him to return after a very brief captivity."

An old man who had visited the British camp at Tate's Place on the 4th, arrived in the American on the morning of the 5th, and gave further information as to the route and condition of the British force; while another cripple spy took stock of the royalists on the afternoon of the 6th, and reported that their numbers did not exceed 1500 men. On the 7th, a third spy, named Gilmer, by passing himself off as a loyalist, obtained from two women of a loyal family the information, "that the youngest had been in Ferguson's camp that very morning, which was only about three miles away, and had carried the British commander some chickens; that he was posted on a ridge between two branches, where some deer-hunters had made a camp last autumn." And finally, shortly before the action began, a youth named Pender was captured riding in great haste. "Colonel Hambright, knowing that this lad had a brother and other relatives in Ferguson's camp, caused his prompt arrest. On searching him, a fresh despatch from Ferguson to Cornwallis was found, manifesting great anxiety as to his situation, and earnestly renewing his request for immediate assistance. . . . Interrogating young Pender as to the kind of dress Ferguson wore, he replied that while that officer was the best uniformed man on the mountain, they could not see his military suit, as he wore a checked shirt or duster over it. Colonel Hambright at once called the attention of his men to this peculiarity of Ferguson's dress. 'Well, poys,' said he in his broken Pennsylvania-German accent, 'when you see dat man mit a pig shirt on over his clothes, you may know who him is, and mark him mit your rifles.'"

At Cowpens on the night of 6th October, the Americans, whose numbers had been 3000 at Gilbert-town, and had since been added to, determined to push on and attack the royalists before they could be relieved. They mounted a large number of their force on horseback, and hurried forward. As to the proportions of the numbers actually engaged, there has been much controversy—American sources generally minimising those of the victors and exaggerating the defeated, while British lay stress upon the disparity. Allaire says that there were 2500 rebels, while Major Ferguson had only 800 men; and General de Peyster, after examining the evidence, and computing the deductions and additions to the assailing force, comes to the conclusion that Allaire states nearly correctly the numbers of the British, and that the Americans had from 1310 to 1370 men in action. Washington Irving distinctly states that the British were outnumbered, and the fact is evident from the character of the fight. "The enemy," says Dr. Ferguson," were in numbers so superior to Ferguson's detachment, and so well acquainted with all the approaches to his position, that they made arrangements to surround him and cut off his retreat." The name of that position ought to have been a good omen. "That portion," writes Draper, "of the oblong hill or stony ridge, now historically famous, is in York County, South Carolina, about a mile and a half south of the North Carolina line. It is some 600 yards long, and about 250 from one base across to the other; or from 60 to 120 wide on the top, tapering to the south—'so narrow,' says Mill's Statistics, 'that a man standing on it may be shot from either side.' Its summit was some sixty* feet above the level of the surrounding country." But strong as in one sense the position was, it was weak as against the particular assailants. It had the fatal defect of Majuba Hill, for its sides afforded cover to attack, and the defenders when surrounded could be swept from either side. Many writers have therefore condemned it as a position. Lossing remarks, "it was a strange place for a camp or a battle," and de Peyster, after condemning the tactics which selected it, and remarking on Ferguson's high opinion of its capability for defence, adds, "It is true he was not driven from it; but its bald rocky summit merely served, like the sacrificial stone of the Aztecs, for the immolation of the victims."† On the other hand, "General Simon Bernard, one of the most distinguished engineers and aides-de-camp of the great Napoleon, and subsequently in the

* "More than 100 feet above above the depressions drained by adjacent streams."—*De Peyster.* The elevation above sea level of the summit is 1500 feet.

† " Still," he says, "in justice to a soldier of so much ability as Ferguson is admitted by friend and foe to have been, the selection of the battle-ground must have been due to some good reason. It is very likely that he chose an open place that he might have the militia under complete and constant supervision."

United States engineer service, on examining the battle-ground of King's Mountain, said, 'The Americans by their victory in that engagement erected a monument to perpetuate the brave men who had fallen there, and the shape of the hill itself would be an eternal monument of the military genius and skill of Colonel Ferguson in selecting a position so well adapted for defence; and that no other plan of assault but that pursued by the mountain men could have succeeded against him." According to Tarleton, Ferguson occupied the best position he could find. He had given his militia a *rendezvous*, and for that purpose it was necessary to select some well-known landmark or town. The country was largely covered with wood, and individual officers, local bands, or even the succour advancing under Tarleton, might easily go astray, lose precious time, or fall into the hands of the backwoodsmen, unless they had a well-defined point to march upon. And having chosen King's Mountain as such a *rendezvous*, and trysted the loyalists to meet him there, Ferguson would feel bound to make the most of his position, even if on arriving he found it not so desirable a tactical one as he had hoped. Apparently there was not in the immediate neighbourhood so large an open space for a camp, and on the hill he was less liable to be surprised. Fulfilling the necessary conditions as a place of lookout for the friends he expected, King's Mountain seems to have been in other respects the best position available.

"The position," writes Washington Irving, "taken by Ferguson was a strong one. King's Mountain rises out of a broken country, and is detached on the north from inferior heights by a deep valley so as to resemble an insulated promontory about half-a-mile in length, with sloping sides excepting on the north. The mountain was covered for the most part with lofty forest trees, free from underwood, interspersed with boulders and masses of grey rock. The forest was sufficiently open to give free passage to horsemen. As the Americans drew nearer, they could occasionally, through the openings of the woodland, descry the glittering of arms along a level ridge forming the crest of King's Mountain. This Ferguson had made his stronghold, boasting that 'if all the rebels in hell should attack him they would not drive him from it.'"

The morning had been wet and stormy, but the weather had

cleared, and it was a beautiful autumn afternoon, when on Saturday, 7th October, the Americans, under the associated colonels, came within striking distance of King's Mountain. Screened by the surrounding forest they dismounted, and formed themselves into at least four main columns. Those on the right and left were to pass round the British position and attack the mountain from the rear, while the two central columns advanced to the assault in front. In this order they arrived within quarter-of-a-mile of the British position before they were discovered. For ten minutes a "furious and bloody battle" was kept up with the two central columns alone, then the others chimed in, and the attack was delivered from all the points of the compass. For fifty-five minutes more the firing was heavy and almost incessant. "The mountain," said one of the American combatants, "was covered with fire and smoke and almost seemed to thunder." The provincials with their bayonets "could make only a momentary impression," and though encouraged by the almost ubiquitous presence of their leader, and gallantly handled under him by Captain de Peyster, their numbers were too few to enable them to follow up the charges that were invariably successful, and they were constantly recalled to meet new assailants. "The British," writes General de Peyster, "depended on their discipline, their manhood, and the bayonet. The Americans took to the trees, shunned anything like personal encounters, and while safe under cover shot down their enemies one by one, just as the Indians of the present day slaughter our troops at the west." Ramsey, the American historian of the Revolution in the Carolinas, who was himself a member of Congress, and wrote after the events he describes, and before the passions of the great struggle had subsided, yet speaks with the highest respect of the British commander, and relates how when the picket was driven in on the main body, "Colonel Ferguson with the greatest bravery ordered his men to charge"; how that charge had no sooner been made with effect, than the Americans, "from an unexpected quarter, poured in a well-directed fire"; how "the British bayonet was again successful, and caused them also to fall back"; and how, when another relay of adversaries "ascended the mountain and renewed the attack from that eminence, Colonel Ferguson, whose conduct was equal to his courage, presented a new front, and was again successful; but all his efforts were unavailing." In all these charges he seems to have had his men perfectly in hand. Having driven back the Americans at the point of the bayonet, they poured a rifle volley after them; and "slowly and with great precision retreated, loading their rifles as they retraced their steps, as they had learnt very skilfully to do by the example and instructions of Ferguson." But in these short retreats they suffered severely from the hidden marksmen in the cover below; and the hunters of the backwoods knew very well that the man who fires from above on his mark, is not likely—owing, it is said, to terrestrial refraction—to make nearly such good practice as he who fires from below. Many of the British bullets rattled over the heads of the Americans, shredding the twigs from the trees; while the loyalists were distinctly seen above, stood exposed in the open, and, owing to their situation on the summit, could be fired at freely from all sides, without fear of the balls passing on into friendly ranks. Thus in every way did the action resemble that on the Majuba, and another evidence of the similarity was the unusual number of the dead who were found shot through the head. But even the raw levies of militia seem to have borne themselves bravely, till demoralised by the fall of their leader, and the gallant little band of Provincials performed prodigies of valour. All the American accounts allow that they broke and chased their enemies down the hill three times; and the tradition of the New York family to which Ferguson's second-in-command belonged, asserts that they drove back their enemies seven times before the final catastrophe occurred.* "Ferguson," writes Washington Irving, "exasperated at being thus hunted into his mountain-fastness, had been chafing in his rocky lair, and meditating a furious sally. He now rushed out with his regulars, made an impetuous charge with the bayonet, and, dislodging his assailants from their coverts, began to drive them down the mountain, they not having a bayonet among them. He had not proceeded far when a flanking fire was opened by one of the other divisions; facing about and attacking this, he was again successful, when a third fire was opened from another quarter.

* It is not without corroboration from Draper's narrative.

Thus, as fast as one division gave way before the bayonet, another came to its relief; while those who had given way, rallied and returned to the charge. The nature of the fighting ground was more favourable to the rifle than the bayonet, and this was a kind of warfare which the frontier men were at home. Ferguson found that he was completely in the hunter's toils; beset on every side, but he stood bravely at bay, until the ground around him was strewed with the killed and wounded, picked off by the fatal rifle. His men were at length broken, and retreated in confusion along the ridge. He galloped from place to place endeavouring to rally them, when a rifle-ball brought him to the ground, and his white horse was seen careering down the mountain without a rider." "Resistance," says Ramsey, "on the part of Colonel Ferguson was in vain; but his unconquerable spirit refused to surrender. After having repulsed a succession of adversaries, pouring in their fire from new directions, this distinguished officer received a mortal wound." "He had," says his biographer, Dr. Adam Ferguson, "two horses killed under him, while he remained untouched himself; but he afterwards received a number of wounds, of which it is said any one was mortal, and, dropping from his horse, expired while his foot yet hung in the stirrup. The spirit which thus refused to be subdued being now no more, the officer on whom the command devolved, though brave and equal to the trust, was compelled to accept of quarter for himself and the few that remained under his command."

Poetic fantasy might find a subject for meditation, in the fact that the device of the House of Hanover, the riderless white horse, should have been the emblem of victory to the rebel host on this well contested field. "The army of mountaineers," observes Washington Irving," were little aware of the importance of the achievement. The battle of King's Mountain, inconsiderable as it was in the numbers engaged, turned the tide of Southern warfare. Just below the forks of the Catawba, the tidings of the defeat reached Tarleton. His party in all haste rejoined Cornwallis. The victory of King's Mountain, which, in its influence on the spirits of the American soldiers, was like the rising at Concord, in its effects like the successes at Bennington, changed the aspect of the war. Cornwallis had hoped to step with ease from one Carolina to another, and from these to the conquest of Virginia—he had now no choice but to retreat."

All annalists agree in bearing testimony to the gallant conduct of the British commander in the battle. Unless one or two of his officers were attached for the purpose of drilling the militia, he was the only man engaged whose home was not on the American side of the Atlantic. De Peyster, quoting another historian, describes him "as riding from one end of his line to the other, encouraging his men to prolong the conflict. With desperate courage he passed from one exposed point to another of equal danger. He carried in his wounded hand a shrill sounding silver whistle, whose signal was universally known through the ranks, was of immense service throughout the battle, and gave a kind of ubiquity to his movements. Rushing from one regiment to another, encouraging some, and directing others; Major Ferguson performed prodigies of valour, when he was shot by an American rifleman, and Captain Abraham de Peyster, of 'the king's American regiment,' a Tory from New York, took the command."

Accounts differ as to the period of the action at which Ferguson fell. Most historians unite in stating that his fall finally determined the issue of the battle, but, on the other hand, Lieutenant Allaire's statement was,—"We lost, early in the action, Major Ferguson of the 71st regiment, a man strongly attached to his king and country, well-informed in the art of war, brave, humane, and an agreeable companion, in short he was universally esteemed in the army, and I have every reason to regret his unhappy fate." Captain Taylor, another Provincial officer, who commanded the small troop of mounted men attached to the force, describes de Peyster, as "behaving like a good brave officer," after the command devolved on him, and "disputing the ground as long as it was possible to defend it against four times our number." And Lenoir, a captain in Winston's band, on the other side, says "Colonel Ferguson had seven or eight bullets shot through him, and fell some time before the battle was over."

But Chesney, who was on Ferguson's staff, and Colonel Shelby, one of the American leaders, are positive that the white flag was hoisted soon after Colonel Ferguson was killed, and such is the language of the official report drawn up by Campbell, Shelby and Cleveland. Campbell says Ferguson was killed "near the close of the action," and a host of independent witnesses, whose testimony is collected by Draper, describe with minuteness the circumstances of his fall when the fight was nearly over. The discrepancy is to be accounted for by the fact that it was some time after the white flag was hoisted, and the surrender made, before the firing ceased, and the wild backwoodsmen were made to comprehend the nature of the transaction termed a capitulation, while, even later on, the rumour that a relieving force was advancing caused them to pour a fierce volley on the defenceless crowd of prisoners. The first man who raised the white flag was shot down, another who was mounted on the same horse, that the emblem might be again clearly seen, met the same fate, and although on a third being hoisted, an American officer proclaimed the surrender, and the loyalists hung out white handkerchiefs on their guns and halberds; "few of the Americans understood the signal, and the few that did chose not to know what it meant, so that even after submission the slaughter continued." One, at least, of the American colonels did his best to stop the butchery, and de Peyster, sitting on his grey horse, indignantly expostulated. It was after the loyalists had been surrounded by a ring four deep, and the conquerors had cheered in honour of their victory, that, on the false alarm of Tarleton's relieving force, or some stray shots by stragglers in the woods, to which some of the Americans attribute the fall of Colonel Williams, the order was given to open the fire, of which a frank American officer says, "we killed near a hundred of the Tories after the surrender of the British, and could hardly be restrained from killing the whole of them."

Draper has gathered many anecdotes and details of much interest about the battle, and the conduct of the British chief. The strife owed its peculiarly embittered character to the fact that relatives and local rivals found themselves fighting as fierce partisans on either side. Indeed, in at least two instances, it is said brothers fell mutually pierced by each others bullets, and it is certain that the same family lost four sons in the battle, two upon each side. In one of the instances in which a brother was killed the marksman had fired at a hole in a tree from which he saw several effective shots proceed, and silenced the loyalist. On examining the spot afterwards he found he had killed one brother and wounded another, and the discovery unhinged his mind. The provincials who had, when first embodied, been clothed in green, but by their services had fully proved their title to the national scarlet, which they wore in the later years of the war, would be conspicuous by their uniform, and the other combatants were distinguished by badges in their hats, the loyalists wearing pine-twigs and the Americans slips of paper. Ferguson had carefully placed his men along the crest of the mountain, with the Rangers on the right, and that gallant band, only 70 strong, bore the brunt of the action, being transferred to charge again and again wherever danger most threatened. For, great as was his skill and love of the rifle, he was always eager to discard it for the bayonet. At the close of the action the provincials only numbered 20 unwounded men. But the local militia did good service as marksmen, and one little band in particular, which Colonel Ferguson had posted among some rock boulders, and judiciously reinforced when their galling fire provoked an attempt to dislodge them, held their ground bravely till near the end of the battle. Upwards of twenty dead loyalists were found jammed among the rocks where they had stationed themselves, who had all been shot directly through the head.

"Such," says Draper, "was the nature of the ground and the thick intervening foliage of the trees, that the Whigs were not discovered till within a quarter of a mile of Ferguson: when the enemy's drums beat to arms, and the shrill whistle of their commander was distinctly heard, notifying his followers to repair to their places in the ranks, and be ready for their work, for they well knew that no child's play was in reserve for them." When the woods on three sides resounded with the fierce Indian war-whoop with which the Americans advanced, and which de Peyster* had heard before at Musgrove's Mills, it is said he remarked to

* It is said that de Peyster, being reflected on at a dinner in Charleston for having surrendered after Ferguson was killed, challenged his critic, and shot him in the duel. He published in the papers a Cartel, offering to meet any one who questioned his conduct. His own life had been saved by a rifle ball that struck him, being intercepted by a doubloon in his pocket, which, bent by the impact, was long preserved in his family. (v App. vii.).

Ferguson, "These things are ominous, these are the d——d yelling boys." "And when these terrific shouts saluted Ferguson's ears he expressed fears for the result." That he may have felt such apprehension is probable, but to express it is surely the last thing he would do, for to his men he was all encouragement. Towards the close of the action, Colonel Hambright, who had been wounded but refused to retire, "exclaimed in his broken German, "Huzza, my brave boys, fight on a few minutes more and the battle will be over." Hearing this encouraging shout, Ferguson, it is said, responded, "Huzza, brave boys, the day is our own." It was among the last of the British leader's utterances to animate his men in a hopeless struggle." Dr. Ramsey, in his "History of Tennesee," asserts that the Tories had begun to show flags in token of surrender even before Ferguson was disabled, seeing which he rode up in two instances and cut them down with his sword. It was "suggested to him by some of his officers that it was useless to prolong the contest and throw their lives away. . . . . But Ferguson's proud heart could not think of surrendering: he despised his enemies, and swore that "he never would yield to such a d——d banditti." At last, according to one account, he determined on a bold effort to break through the encircling line of fire at the head of his few troopers. De Peyster's Rangers had again been ordered to the south-western extremity of the mountain, where two of the American bodies were pressing the militia, and before reaching the point where their services were most required, had to pass through a blaze of rifle-fire from the side-slopes, losing many men as they went. The small corps of cavalry under Lieutenant Taylor, consisting of twenty men made up from the Rangers, were then ordered to mount, and ride forward to aid de Peyster, but as fast as they mounted they were picked off by the American marksmen. Then it is said that Ferguson, accompanied by two loyalist field officers, all mounted, made a bold dash at the enemy, but fell as he reached the rebel line, while his companions, Colonel Husband and Major Plummer, were shot down as they attempted to retreat.

"At length," writes Draper, "satisfied that all was lost, and firmly resolving not to fall into the hands of the despised 'Backwater men,' Ferguson, with a few chosen friends, made a desperate attempt to break through the Whig lines on the southeastern side of the mountain and escape. The intrepid British leader made a bold dash for life and freedom, with his sword in his left hand cutting and slashing until he had broken it."* Before the action began, "the admonition had gone from soldier to soldier, 'Look out for Ferguson, with his sword in his left hand, and wearing a light hunting shirt.' One of Sevier's men attempted to arrest the career of the great leader, but his gun snapped, when he called out to Robert Young of the same regiment, 'There's Ferguson, shoot him.' Young discharged his rifle, when Ferguson fell from his horse, and his associates were either killed or driven back. Several rifle bullets had taken effect on Ferguson, apparently about the same time, and a number claimed the honour of having shot the fallen chief. Certain it is that Ferguson received six or eight wounds, one of them through the head. He was unconscious when he fell and did not long survive."

In the traditions of the region, the fall of the British commander has assumed an almost mythological character. It has been said that he met in mortal combat, Colonel Williams, the senior in rank of the American officers, said to have had a Brigadier's commission in his pocket, whom the British regarded as commanding in the action, and that both fell as their swords crossed. Some of the accounts almost realize the description of the encounter of Mamilius and Herminius at the battle of Lake Regillus :—

> "All round them paused the battle,
> While met in mortal fight,
> The Roman and the Tusculan,
> The horses black and white . . .
> And side by side these chiefs of pride
> Together down fell dead—
> Fast, fast, with heels wild spurning,
> The milk-white charger fled."

But the traditions of an imaginative people must be received with

---

* "Colonel Shelby mentions the sword incident, and Benjamin Sharp corroborates it, while several others unite in testifying to the fact that he spurred his horse and rushed out, attempting to escape."

caution,* and the story of King's Mountain, the wild backwoods-

* This tradition is, however, corroborated by Colonel Ferguson's Assistant-Adjutant-General, Alexander Chesney, whose testimony as an eye-witness of the action may be added to those already collected. " King's Mountain from its height would have enabled us to oppose a superior force with advantage, had it not been covered with wood, which sheltered the Americans and enabled them to fight in their favourite manner. In fact, after driving in our picquets, they were enabled to advance in three divisions, under separate leaders, to the crest of the hill in perfect safety, until they took post, and opened an irregular but destructive fire from behind trees and other cover. Colonel Cleveland's was first perceived, and repulsed by a charge made by Colonel Ferguson; Colonel Selby's next, and met a similar fate, being driven down the hill; lastly, the detachment under Colonel Campbell, and, by desire of Colonel Ferguson, I presented a new front which opposed it with success. By this time the Americans who had been repulsed had regained their former stations, and, sheltered behind trees, poured in an irregular destructive fire. In this manner the engagement was maintained near an hour, the mountaineers flying when there was danger of being charged by the bayonet, and returning again so soon as the British detachment had faced about to repel another of their parties. Colonel Ferguson was at last recognised by his gallantry, although wearing a hunting shirt, and fell, pierced by seven balls, at the moment he had killed the American Colonel Williams with his left hand, the right being useless. I had just relieved the troops a second time by Ferguson's orders, when Captain de Peyster succeeded to the command. He soon after sent out a flag of truce: but as the Americans renewed their fire afterwards, ours was also renewed under the supposition that they would give no quarter; and a dreadful havoc took place until the flag was sent out a second time; then the work of destruction ceased. The Americans surrounded us with double lines, and we grounded arms with the loss of one third of our number.

. . . At Gilbertstown a mock trial was held, and twenty-four sentenced to death; ten of them suffered before the approach of Tarleton's loyalist cavalry force obliged our captors to move towards the Yadkin, cutting and striking us by road in a savage manner. Colqnel Cleveland then offered to enlarge me, on condition that I would teach his regiment, for one month, the exercise practised by Colonel Ferguson, which I refused, although he swore I should suffer death for it when we got to Moravian town. Happily his threat was not put to the test, as I had the good fortune to make my escape one evening when close to that place."

As Colonel Tarleton's narrative, in his work on the campaigns of 1780 and 1781, is that of the officer in command of the force sent too late to the relief, corroborates in the main the American accounts, and is at one with the hostile annalists in its estimate of the importance of the battle, it may also be quoted. "The Americans," he says, "selected 1600 chosen men on horseback for a vigorous pursuit. The rapid march of this corps soon rendered

men, and Ferguson's Tory followers, have afforded much scope for lovers of the marvellous.

"It is proper," observes Draper, "to advert briefly to Ferguson's conduct in the battle. It was that of a hero. He did all that mortal man could have done, under the circumstances, to avert the impending catastrophe. He was almost ubiquitous—his voice, his presence, and his whistle, everywhere animated his men, either to renew their bayonet charges, or maintain a firm stand against the steadily encroaching mountaineers. But he trusted too much to the bayonet against an enemy as nimble as the antelope." And, unfortunately, as "the famous cavalry Colonel, Harry Lee," observed of the battlefield,—"it was more assailable by the rifle than defensible by the bayonet."

"As long," continues Draper, "as Ferguson lived, his unyielding spirit scorned to surrender. He persevered until he received his mortal wounds. His fall very naturally disheartened his followers. For some time before the fatal event, there was really nothing to encourage them, save the faintest hope, which they vainly cherished, of momentary relief from Tarleton. Animated by the brave example of their heroic leader, and still confiding in his fruitful military resources, they had maintained the unequal contest under all disadvantages. Losing his inspiration, they lost all—with him perished the last hope of success."

"Most of the accounts represent that the British colonel was killed outright. He is said to have received six or eight bullet-holes in his body—one penetrating his thigh, another reshattering his right arm just above the elbow; and yet he continued to raise his sword in his left hand, till a rifle ball piercing his head, put an end to further fighting or consciousness. In falling from his horse, or while being conveyed to the rear a silver whistle dropped from

an action inevitable. Major Ferguson heard of the enemies' approach at King's Mountain; he occupied the most favourable position he could find, and waited the attack. The action commenced at four o'clock in the afternoon of the 7th October, and was disputed with great bravery near an hour, when the death of the gallant Ferguson threw his whole corps into total confusion. No effort was made after this event to resist the enemy's barbarity, or to revenge the fall of their leader. . . . . The destruction of Ferguson and his corps marked the period and the extent of the first expedition into North Carolina."

his vest pocket, which was picked up by one of his soldiers, Elias Powell, who preserved it for many years; and Powell and three others were seen at the close of the surrender, bearing off in a blanket their fallen chief to a spring near the mountain's brow, on the southern side of the elevation; and there gently bolstered him up with rocks and blankets. One of the Tories (?) who had just grounded his gun, taking in the situation, and true to his plundering instincts, ran up, and was in the act of thrusting his hand into the dying man's pockets, when the unfeeling intruder was repelled by one of the attendants, who, rudely pushing him away, exclaimed with a sarcastic oath,—'Are you going to rob the dead?' A little after, Colonel Shelby rode up, and thinking perhaps that Ferguson might yet be sensible of what was said to him, though he evidently was not, exclaimed—'Colonel, the fatal blow is struck, we've burgoyned you!' The life of this restless British leader soon ebbed away." . . . "So curious were the Whigs to see the fallen British chief, that many repaired to the spot to view his body as it lay in its gore and glory. Lieutenant Samuel Johnson of Cleveland's regiment desired to be carried there, that he too might look upon the dying or lifeless leader of the enemy, whom he had so valiantly fought, when Colonel Cleveland and two of the soldiers bore the wounded lieutenant to the place of pilgrimage, and even the transfixed Robert Henry, amid his pains and sufferings could not repress his anxiety to take a look at Ferguson. It was probably where he was conveyed and breathed his last that he was buried—on the south-eastern declivity of the mountain, where his mortal remains, wrapped not in a military cloak, or hero's coffin, but in a raw beef's hide found a peaceful sepulture."

But even this was for some time denied, and it is doubtful, whether the delayed burial took place on the hillside, which had been so bravely defended. "The victors," says de Peyster, "remained upon the field the night of the battle: the next day, the 8th, was Sunday. The dead were buried at dawn, but not all; one at least was left to the birds and beasts of prey." Colonel Tarleton, who had been despatched by Lord Cornwallis, with the light infantry, the British legion and a three-pounder to Ferguson's relief, and thus had special opportunities of investigating the "mortifying news of his melancholy fate," says—"the mountaineers, it is reported, used every insult and indignity, after the action, towards the dead body of Major Ferguson, and exercised horrid cruelties on the prisoners that fell into their possession." Draper quotes his statement with the words—"some of the more thoughtless of the Whig soldiery committed an act which we would fain be excused from the pain of recording." But the fact does not rest on Tarleton's statement alone. Colonel Hanger, who was then serving in the British legion, records that "the Americans had such an inveteracy against Ferguson, that they buried all the other bodies, but stripped Ferguson's of its clothes, and left it on the field of battle, to be devoured by the turkey-buzzards, a species of vulture in that country." And Dr. Ferguson tells the same tale, with an additional circumstance that alleviates its painful character. "The body lay stripped on the ground, while the men lately under his command, now prisoners of war, desired leave to bury his remains, with what they termed the honours of a soldier's grave; but this request, addressed to the recent feelings of a ferocity, which resented the opposition even of the most generous enemy, was refused. This token of respect and affection, however, was paid to the deceased by the inhabitants of a neighbouring village, who, having experienced his humanity, gave the body a decent interment in their own burying-ground."

The conquerors, expecting to be assailed by Tarleton and his fiery horsemen, hastened rapidly away; a scanty burial was given to the dead, while "many of the wounded were seen upon the ground two days after the battle, imploring a little water to cool their burning tongues, but they were left to perish there, and this long hill was whitened with their bones." Vultures and wolves flocked to the place, and "so bold and audacious did the latter grow, that they, in some instances, showed a disposition to attack the living, when visiting the scene of battle. And, long after the war, it is said that King's Mountain was the favourite resort of the wolf hunter."

"Many a souvenir," writes Draper, "was appropriated by the victors. Captain Joseph McDowell, of Pleasant Garden, secured some of Ferguson's table service—six of his china dinner plates, and a small coffee cup and saucer; several of which interesting war-trophies are yet retained among his descendants. Colonel

Shelby obtained the fallen chieftain's famous silver whistle, while the smaller one fell to the lot of Elias Powell; and Colonel Sevier secured his silken sash and lieutenant-colonel's commission and de Peyster's sword; Colonel Campbell secured at least a portion of his correspondence. Ferguson's white charger, who had careered down the mountain, when his master was shot from his back, was by general consent assigned to the gallant Colonel Cleveland, who was too unwieldy to travel on foot, and who had lost his horse in the action. Samuel Talbot, turning over Ferguson's dead body, picked up his pistol, which had dropped from his pocket. His large silver watch, as round as a turnip, fell into the hands of one of Lacey's men; and Dr. Moore, in his 'Life of Lacey,' says he frequently saw it; that it traded for about 45 or 50 dollars as a curiosity." A Captain Lewis "secured some of the British commander's arms,—one a jewel-hilted poniard, which he retained many years." As Ferguson was Major of a Highland regiment, it is probable that this "jewel-hilted poniard" was a cairngorm mounted dirk. "His sword was picked up on the ground, and, according to one account, it passed into Colonel Cleveland's possession, but with more probability, according to others, it fell into the hands of Colonel Sevier." It is said that there was found on his body a letter from Col. Cruger, at Ninety-six, dated October 3rd, in which he said—"I flattered myself they (the militia) would have been equal to the mountain lads, and that no further call for the defensive would be made on this part of the Province. I begin to think our views for the present rather large. We have been led to this probably in expecting too much from the militia."

The battle of King's Mountain has not unfrequently inspired poets of various calibre in the United States. A rough ballad on the battle was sung in the Carolinas, and the following lines are taken from a spirited lay that appeared in 1860 *

* "King's Mountain, a ballad of the Carolinas"—"Harper's Monthly Magazine," October, 1860, vol. xxi., p. 670. The ballad is illustrated with a sketch of the battle ground, and what is termed Colonel Ferguson's tomb, though. curiously enough, the legend inscribed on it does not bear that he was interred below. "The battle," it is said, "took place in South Carolina, but only a-mile-and-a-half south of the North Carolina line. Colonel Ferguson was

"And soon to the eyes of our yeomen,
  All panting with rage at the sight
Gleamed the long wavy tents of the foeman,
  As he lay in his camp on the height.
Grim dashed they away as they bounded,
  The hunters to hem in the prey,
And with Deckard's long rifles surrounded,
  Then the British rose fast to the fray :
And never with arms of more vigour
  Did their bayonets press through the strife,
Where with every swift pull of the trigger
  The sharpshooters dashed out a life.
'Twas the meeting of eagles and lions,
  'Twas the rushing of tempests and waves,
Insolent triumph 'gainst patriot defiance,
  Born freemen 'gainst sycophant slaves.
Scotch Ferguson sounding his whistle,
  As from danger to danger he flies,
Feels the moral that lies in Scotch thistle,
  With its 'touch me who dare,' and he dies!"

Another dark touch is added to the picture, by the following account of a visit paid the scene, in an article of 1862 on "American Historical Trees"*:—"viii. The Tory Tulip-Tree.— On a dismal morning in January, 1849, I crossed the dividing line between North and South Carolina, near the Broad River. A chilling north-east wind, freighted with sleet, was driving over the dreary country, and wet snow, two inches deep, covered the ground. I was on my way to King's Mountain. . . . . I arrived near the battle-ground in the afternoon, when the clouds were breaking, and on horseback, accompanied by a resident in the neighbourhood, ascended the pleasant wooded hills to the memorable spot. The sun was low in the west, and its slant rays,

---

one of the most distinguished of the British partizan warriors in America during the Revolution. He was specially opposed as a great leader of riflemen to the southern riflemen; was himself an inventor of an improved rifle which in that day gained him large reputation. His bravery was remarkable as well as his skill. During the battle he used a silver whistle, which was to be heard sounding everywhere through all the din of the conflict. The Tory chiefs were executed on the spot soon after the battle. Tradition says that ten were hung from the tree that appears on the right in our view of the battle ground."

* "Harper's Monthly Magazine," vol. xxiv., p. 730.

gleaming through the boughs dripping with the melted snows, garnished the forest for a few moments with all the seeming splendour of the mines. In a little dell at the northern foot of the hill, whereon most of the battle was fought, was a clear brook laving the roots of an enormous tulip-tree whose branches were widespread. 'That,' said Mr. Leslie, my companion, 'we call the Tory tulip-tree, because, after the battle here, ten Tories were hung upon these two lower branches.' 'Were they not prisoners of war?' I asked. 'They were taken in battle,' he replied, 'but they were too wicked to live.' . . . . Near that tree in the lonely hollow of the solitary mountains, is an humble monument to mark the spot where the American officers and Ferguson, the leader of the Tories who were slain in battle, were buried." One inscription reads, "Colonel Ferguson, an officer belonging to his Britannic Majesty, was here defeated and killed." Probably local tradition has transferred to the locality of the fight the incident that really occured at Gilbert-town a week after the battle. Yet, in view of the deeds which more than justified Ferguson's designation of "barbarians," and warning to the loyalists in the neighbourhood, there may have been more hanging where the action took place. It is certain that a few days after the battle a party of Whigs, hunting for horses in the vicinity, descried one of the Tory foragers or fugitives who had escaped in the meleé, and had ventured to revisit the scene, caught him, and promptly suspended him from the branch of a tree, where his body hung till it could hang no longer. This may have given the tree its name, and near Gilbert-town there is shown the Gallows Oak. It may be that among those who thus perished were some who might be liable to the designation of "horse thieves," but it is certain that others suffered for "no crime but that of loyalty."* When the news of

---

* The conquerors were especially bitter towards the officers of the militia. So strong was the sentiment of loyalty in North Carolina that Colonel Williams had been defeated in the election as State Senator of 1778, by "the strong Tory influence in his section," and Colonel Cleveland, "who," says de Peyster, "was noted for his great severity—to use a mild expression—towards the unhappy loyalists who fell into his power," and belonged to that State, has been credited with the chief advocacy of cruel measures. Colonel Mills, the sufferer of highest rank, was also from North Carolina, and is described by de Peyster as "bearing a very high character," and by Draper as "a man of fair reputa-

the disaster reached the British headquarters at Charlotte it produced a deep impression on all. An American partisan of reckless character, who was a prisoner, indulged with the liberty of the town, overhearing it told by one officer of the guard to another, leapt on a pile of wood, and imitating the crowing of a cock, exclaimed, "Day is at hand." All historians agree in recognizing how materially King's Mountain had altered the aspect of affairs. It prevented the invasion of Virginia, unhinged the completed conquest of the Carolinas, and was the first of the untoward events that culminated at Yorktown.

The death of Ferguson was fatal to the scheme into which he had thrown himself so heartily, for the loyalists deprived of the leader whom they loved, and disheartened by the defeat and the terrible butchery which had followed it, never rose again with the same alacrity; and the Americans were everywhere inspirited by the event, over which their intercepted letters showed them exulting, with more delight than dignity, as the fall of "the famous Ferguson." The tone of jubilation which naturally enough pervaded their despatches, shows that the full significance of the victory was appreciated by their generals, if not by those who won it.

tion." Allaire notes in his diary of 14th October. "Twelve officers were chosen to try the militia prisoners, particularly those who had the most influence in the country. They condemned thirty. In the evening they began to execute Lieut.-Colonel Mills, Capt. Wilson, Capt. Chitwood, and six others, who unfortunately fell a sacrifice to their infamous mock jury." "These brave but unfortunate loyalists with their latest breath expressed their unutterable detestation of the rebels, and of their base and infamous proceedings: and, as they were being turned off, extolled their king and the British Government. Mills, Wilson, and Chitwood died like Romans." Though there had undoubtedly been many irregularities committed by marauding bands on both sides, in the course of a civil strife peculiarly embittered, it is remarkable that Colonel Campbell issued an order, some days after King's Mountain, in which he described "the plundering parties who issue out of the camp and indiscriminately rob both Whig and Tory," as "leaving our friends in a worse situation than the enemy would have done." Allaire mentions that on one occasion the captives were treated to a sermon "stuffed as full of Republicanism as their camp is of horse-thieves." The prisoners were shockingly maltreated, and the orders to their guard were, if Tarleton's force appeared, first to shoot down the officers, and then to fire upon the rest.

The following are the official accounts, on both sides, from the Annual Register of the time :—

"America.—New York, Nov. 30. After the battle of Camden Lord Cornwallis advanced into North Carolina; and Colonel Ferguson, attempting to join him from Ninety-six with about 400 militia, was attacked at King's Mountain by near 2000 rebels. He twice repulsed them, and went out with 30 men to reconnoitre, when he was unfortunately killed. This dispirited his party; the rebels made a third attack and succeeded. They killed and took upwards of 300.* This stroke obliged Lord Cornwallis to retire into South Carolina."

The "New Jersey Gazette," of October 25, contains the following account:

"Camp, Rocky River, Oct. 10.
"Sir,
"I have the pleasure of handing you very agreeable intelligence from the west. Ferguson, the great partisan, has miscarried. That we are assured by Mr. Tate, brigade-major in General Sumpter's late command; the particulars from that gentleman's mouth stand thus: Colonels Campbell, Cleveland, Shelby, Seveer, Williams, Brandon, Lacy, &c., formed a conjunct body near Gilbert-town, consisting of 2000. From this body were selected 1600 good horse, who immediately went in pursuit of Colonel Ferguson, who was making his way to Charlotte. Our people overtook him well posted on King's Mountain, and on the evening of the 7th instant, began the attack which continued forty-seven minutes. Colonel Ferguson fell in the action, besides 150 of his men; 810 were made prisoners, including the British— 150 of the prisoners are wounded, 1500 stand of arms fell into our hands. Colonel Ferguson had about 1400 men. Our people surrounded them, and the enemy surrendered. We lost about 40 men, among whom is Major Chronicle of Lincoln County.

* Both British and American sources erred as to Ferguson's force, it being nearly the mean between the estimates or 900-950. Ferguson's Rangers available as infantry, were about 70 men. 20 acted as cavalry, and 10 were assigned to the baggage waggons. Allaire states the loss at 18 of the rangers killed and 33 wounded: of the militia, 100 killed and 90 wounded. Prisoners—64 rangers, including mounted men and wounded; 600 militia. Rebel loss— Brigadier-General Williams, 135 killed; wounded, "equal to ours." The American figures make both the numbers and the loss of the British greater; but various sources differ widely, and the official account was avowedly concocted "to give tone to public report."

Colonel Williams is mortally wounded. The number of our wounded cannot be ascertained. This blow will certainly affect the British very considerably. The brigade-major who gives this was in the action. The above is true. The blow is great. I give you joy on the occasion.

"I am, &c.,

"Hon. Gen. Sumner."

"(Signed)   William Davison.

"Camp, Yadkin Ford, Oct. 10, 1780,
"Eight o'clock evening.

"Sir,

"With great satisfaction I inform you of the defeat of Major Ferguson on King's Mountain, 4 o'clock, Saturday afternoon. The particulars I enclose you as I received them a few minutes ago; also a letter from General Davison of his securing 29 barrels of powder, which were secreted some time since near Charlotte.   "I am, &c.,

"(Signed)   Jathro Sumner."

"Published by order of Congress."

General Gates, in enclosing these despatches, spoke of "the great and glorious news" they contained, and observed, "We are now more than even with the enemy."

When the report of Ferguson's death reached his friends, they were not surprised and scarcely required confirmation. "If not now," they said, "it must be soon, in the continual danger to which he exposes himself." "He had estimated the part which became him to act, as the leader of such parties as were hitherto put under his command; in such services he conceived that he was not only to project what should be done, but to lead in the execution of it. His courage was considerate and calm. He says in a letter to a friend, "I thank God more for this than for all His other blessings, that in every call of danger or honour, I have felt myself collected and equal to the occasion." Anxious to reconcile his parents to the risks to which he was so frequently exposed, he makes the following observation—"The length of our lives is not at our own command, however much the manner of them may be. If our Creator enable us to act the part of men of honour, and to conduct ourselves with spirit, probity, and humanity, the change to another world, whether now or fifty years hence, will not be for the worse." Of the millions," continues the eminent philosopher who has left us so interesting a sketch of the soldier's life, "who were born on the same day as Colonel Ferguson, the longest liver will die at no great interval of time, and none in a manner more worthy of the part which Providence had assigned him to act." Some time must now have passed since the last survivor disappeared from the scene; was there any whose career has been requited by such admiration as his has extorted from the patriotic American historian, writing a century after the crack of the backwoodsmen's rifles signalized the assurance of American Independence?

For long the exploits of Ferguson and Tarleton formed stirring themes of conversation in very distant and different circles. If all accounts be true, they shared—and Tarleton perhaps deserved it—a similar position, in the legends of the Carolinas, to that occupied by Scanderbeg in the traditions of the Turks, by the Cid Campeador in the minds of the Moors, or "the bluidy Claverse" in the imaginations of the Cameronians of the West of Scotland. Their deeds were the subject of many tales told in winter evenings, in log huts and plantations, by the descendants of those whose neighbours had, as "raw levies of the loyal militia, followed Ferguson with the utmost spirit and confidence."

Tarleton, on the other hand, having been noted as a scourge of Whigs in the Colonies, spent his later days as an ally of factious Whigs in Britain. "He* had not long returned from the American War, full of wild stories about Marion, 'the Swamp Fox,' Charles Lee, whom the Indians called 'Boiling Water,' and Sumpter,† the most daring of guerillas, before he was admitted into the social circle of the Prince of Wales. He was an admirable *raconteur*, and many were the stirring anecdotes about the woods and swamps of the western world, with which he regaled his delighted hearers." In these his old companion-in-arms had a prominent place. Tarleton, who has elsewhere recorded his belief that his friend's disaster was not owing to any want of judgment on his part, but was unavoidable, "in spite of his prudent plan of verging towards the royal army," "always believed that the death of Ferguson was the greatest misfortune to the British cause. Certain it is that after his fall in 1780, the loyalists of the Carolinas, who were many

---

* *Vide* Article in "Blackwood's Magazine," October, 1874.
† Sumpter's appellation was "the Game Cock."

times more numerous than their disaffected compatriots, could never again be induced to show fight. About this enterprising soldier, Tarleton had a lot of stories which delighted the guests gathered round the royal supper-table. He would narrate how Ferguson, creeping through the woods upon his belly, would pick off rebels, and reload his weapon with a celerity which commanded the respect of men trained to compete with the Red Indian savages in cypress swamps and tangled thickets of 'black jacks,' or dwarf oaks. It was even asserted"—and here the narrator has considerably under-rated the radical nature of Ferguson's invention—"that he had invented and always used a rifle, anticipating the invention of the percussion cap, which, although perfected by the Rev. Mr. Forsyth in 1807, was not introduced into the British army until the campaign of Sir Charles James Napier against Scinde in 1840. The savage and romantic warfare in which Tarleton and Ferguson played such conspicuous parts, afforded matter for endless stories, of which the Prince Regent was never tired."

Other estimates, written by those who had served along with him, have been preserved, which show how esteemed Ferguson had been by his comrades. One of them writes "that in private life his humanity and benevolence were conspicuous, his friendship steady and sincere. To a distinguished capacity for planning the greatest designs, he added the ardour necessary to carry them into execution; his talent for enterprise attracted the notice of the whole army. Military tactics had been his early and favourite study; considered as a scholar, his genius was solid, his comprehension clear, and his erudition extensive." And General Stuart of Garth, in his book on the "Highlanders and the Highland Regiments," has this notice,—"Major Ferguson was brother to Pitfour. He was appointed Major to Fraser's Highlanders, but commanded a corps of riflemen which bore his name. He possessed original genius, was ardent and enthusiastic, and considered as visionary by the disciples of the mechanical school of war. By zeal, animation, and a liberal spirit, he gained the confidence of the mass of the people, and laid foundations, on which the loyally disposed, who were numerous in the Southern Provinces, would have been organised and disciplined and greatly outnumbered the disaffected. No man in that army was better qualified for such a task ; his ardour was not to be checked by common difficulties. Directing the conduct of men unaccustomed to strict discipline ; instead of commanding obedience, silence, and close attention to the routine of duty, he, with an address, which none but a man who studies and applies the principle, which regulates the actions of the human mind, could be supposed to possess, led them step by step to accomplish the duties of experienced soldiers. At King's Mountain he was overpowered by numbers, and fought and fell like a Spartan."

Dr. Ferguson has preserved the following "of many poetical effusions that appeared in the public prints." They have quite the ring of the 18th century :—

> " Here soldiers sighing o'er a hero's grave,
> Tell how he fought and died—here Genius bends,
> Mourning the patriot worth she could not save,
> While Social Virtue weeps the best of friends."

> "Here bleeding Pity, viewing what is done,
> In silent woe laments her darling son :
> For ne'er a milder warrior thus was laid,—
> His generous breast no evil e'er repaid :
> His heart no selfish passion ever felt,
> For there the chastest love of glory dwelt.
> His martial ardour tend'rest feelings crown'd,
> And, but too daring, not a fault was found.
> Let Honour pay the debt his actions claim ;
> Let candour give to future time his fame ;
> Let grateful Britain to her children just,
> With never fading laurel shade his dust :
> His gallant deeds her youthful soldiers tell,—
> Teach them, like Him, in glory to excel :
> For this he fought ; For this, alas, he fell !"

It is remarkable that more than a century after his death, it should be possible to collect so much detailed information as to the life of a soldier who attained no high military rank, and never commanded a complete regiment in the field. It is emphatic evidence of the impression made in favourable circumstances by personal character, and of the ultimate credit that is won by untiring devotion to duty. But passing from the British records which speak of an active and intelligent officer, enterprising in his profession, and popular among his friends, to American annals, we seem to step into a different atmosphere altogether. We are dealing with the heroic age of a new born nation, and the possibilities of the future invest all who acted even comparatively restricted parts, with a certain dignity and grandeur. The fathers of their country always loom large, and so must the antagonists, whom by the merest chance they defeated. There is a special picturesqueness in the contest waged à l'outrance in the Carolinas, and the phase of it that was enacted in the interior districts, has a completeness of its own. There is something peculiarly fascinating in the fortunes of the expedition, in which a solitary British officer did great things with loyal Americans alone, and which gathered up in brief compass so much that was vital in experiment and in result. But amid all the varied types of character, Provincial soldiers, and hunters of the mountains, loyal gentlemen of high Colonial position, and strong-willed Republican Colonels, wild gaunt backwoodsmen, with long matted hair, bearing the deadly small-bore rifle, and the merciless tomahawk, and the gang of horsestealers, plunderers, and avengers of private grudges, who hang on the skirts of every army in civil strife, there stands out alone, on a level of its own, the personality of the brave soldier of "generous disposition and conciliating manners," who represented the British Crown and the Imperial connection. As Hector is the hero of the Iliad, although Homer wrote from the side of the Greeks, so in the pages which American patriotism has devoted to "King's Mountain and its Heroes," the Scotsman remains the "King of the mountain." It was said of Lord Chatham, that no soldier ever left his presence without feeling himself a braver man when he came out than when he went in, and a similar influence seems to have been exerted by Ferguson on the loyal men of the Southern States. Undoubtedly those who met "like Romans" so terrible a doom, faced a worse fate than his, none the less bravely on account of their intercourse with one, in all whose utterances we seem to hear "the ringing of the Roman tread." Yet, in his character, classic fortitude was blended with the softer spirit of mediæval chivalry, science co-operated with valour, and study came to the aid of genius. If Tarleton, *si parvos licet componere magnis* might be called the Claverhouse of the Carolinas, there was not a little in Ferguson that recalls the temperament and character of Montrose. Had his life been longer spared, he might have been of great service to his country, at a time when she was sorely in want of military genius, and found a happier field for the exercise of riper experience in the days of the great war. But he was

> "Snatched in manhood's prime,
> Though not before the goal of honour won ;
> Swift was the course, but short the time to run !
> Oh ! narrow circle, but of power divine,
> Scanted in space, but perfect in thy line !"

Very wide is the field of reflection opened up by the incident with Washington, and the influence of the action of King's Mountain. Had the events been different, would the opportunity vouchsafed have been met in the spirit which goaded Franklin into irreconcilable malignity, or by the generous policy of the Pitts ! But what a foundation might have been laid for that great scheme of Imperial federation, which has been the dream of the best of British statesmen ? There is nothing more marvellous in history, nothing more full of comfort for the future, than the manner in which the energy of Britons built up another Colonial Empire in Australasia, and a great dominion in India, to replace the one that was lost, but had there never been the severance, what might not united efforts have accomplished ? How much easier would have been the burden of maintaining the independence of Europe against Napoleon ; if indeed the French Revolution had ever been written in the characters of blood that stain the pages of last century. The House of Bourbon paid dear for patronising insurrection in America, and France and Europe paid heavily for the contagious frenzy that swelled the strong and sure current of reform into the revolutionary torrent. We in Britain have scarce recovered from the evils unavoidably resulting from the necessary postponement of developments required by the national growth, which the younger Pitt seemed born to guide, and which might have been accomplished with little friction and more permanent benefit quarter of a century sooner, but for the fatal influence of French Jacobinism upon British political life. But such speculations travel far beyond the incidents that awake them, and we bid farewell to one who, from his first dash of boyish valour on the plains of Germany, down to the mournful, but not inglorious close, in the shade of the Tory tulip-tree on the slope of King's Mountain, far from the old kirk of Deer, or his father's resting-place in the Greyfriars at Edinburgh, maintained the character of a *chevalier sans peur et sans reproche.*

"THE TORY TULIP-TREE."

"The esteem and affection of his brother officers dictated the following epitaph," which was inserted in the "New York Gazette," of 14th February, 1781 :—

"IF AN ARDENT THIRST FOR MILITARY FAME,
A SOCIAL AND BENEVOLENT HEART,
AN UNCOMMON GENIUS,
A MIND GLOWING WITH PATRIOTIC FIRE,
REPLETE WITH USEFUL KNOWLEDGE,
AND CAPABLE
OF PERSEVERING UNDER DIFFICULTIES
WHERE GLORY WAS IN VIEW,
CLAIM OUR ADMIRATION;
THE FATE OF
MAJOR PATRICK FERGUSON,
WHO POSSESSED THESE AND OTHER VIRTUES
IN AN EMINENT DEGREE,
AND WHO FELL
WARRING AGAINST DISCORD,
IRRESISTIBLY
CLAIMS OUR TEARS."

III.

A JACOBITE LAIRD AND HIS FORBEARS.

The Forbeses of Blackton.

"Oh! never shall we know again
   A heart so stout and true,
The olden times have passed away,
   And weary are the new;
The fair white rose has faded
   From the garden where it grew,
And no fond tears, save those of heaven,
   The lonely grave bedew
     Of the last Old Scottish Cavalier
     All of the olden time."
—W. E. AYTOUN.

A JACOBITE LAIRD AND HIS FORBEARS.

"The Whigs may scoff, the Whigs may jeer,
But oh that love maun be sincere,
Which still keeps true whate'er betide,
An' for his sake flings a' beside."
—*Lady Nairne.*

"Lost are our homes, exile and death
Scatter the loyal men :
Yet ere the sword cool in its sheath
Charlie will come again."
—*Skye Boat Song.*

UNINVITING as legal documents and old papers look, there is a rich harvest of romance to be reaped from their study. Not only is this true of the records of those houses that played an important part in their country's annals; the careful student of the past will not despise the gleanings of smaller fields and retired repositories. For, buried among accounts and sasines, and rentals, he may come across some little fact that reveals much of the life of a bygone time, and may stumble on evidence at first-hand forcibly illustrating the struggles of the past. History is the generalized record of the sum of human experience, and it is well, sometimes, not merely to examine the local events that form its less conspicuous shades, but even occasionally to trace out the individual thread of a family's fortunes. It enables us better to realize the sequence of events; it impresses upon us their bearing on the comfort and the welfare of individual men. It may reveal the existence of what the formal historian has overlooked: it is bound to yield the interest, and waken the sympathy which the story of human striving and suffering rarely fails to inspire. It is at worst a harmless indulgence of the industrious curiosity which sends Bolingbroke's Dutch traveller to copy an epitaph, and where an ancient name has come to an end in shadow, it is but becoming that those in whose veins there runs somewhat of its blood should take the trouble to reverently gather and see enshrined the scattered memorials it has left.

Working among the contents of an old charter chest some time ago, we came upon a few papers tied up by themselves, and bearing, when examined, to relate to another name than that whose fortunes we were tracing. Further and closer examination added to them a large manuscript in a quaint old hand, dated in the stirring year 1745, and the personality to whom they had belonged acquired a stronger hold on the imagination from a pair of old silver shoe-buckles tied up along with them. There was, too, a quaint and capacious old snuff box, with a coat of arms upon it, and the same bearings identified as the same owner's a venerable carved oak chair. Curiosity aroused, tradition came to aid; but had it not, the key to unlock the past was supplied by the maligned "science" of heraldry. A study of the old manuscript proved the truth of what a novelist would have been only too ready to imagine, that in that old chair had sat, refreshing himself from the emblazoned snuff-mull, and decorated with these self-same buckles, a gallant champion of the White Rose, who had done what he could to bring "the auld Stuarts back again," who had faced an English jury at Carlisle, and who had found that loyal service to an exiled king was not the line of life best suited to "keep the rigs together." More careful collection of the straws of information that are to be gathered in the antiquarian acres of the Spalding Club, increased the interest the vision of the old Laird had aroused, for it indicated that not only was he a typical Aberdeenshire Jacobite himself, but also the last representative of the Cavalier branch of a great Covenanting house. Strange that in the great Civil War a Forbes should have severed himself from his chief and kinsmen, and been found with the Gordons, his hereditary foes, at the Trot of Turriff in arms for the king. And yet so it was, and high monarchical principles distinguished to the last the branch of Blackton. There was something fascinating and mournful—and the old scraps of musty paper that told the tale seemed almost sacred in our eyes—in the picture of the last of the line, after he had been forced to part with the ancestral home, dragging out the long declining years of his life, in the neighbourhood of friends, but feeling that for him and his the play was closed. Once there came an awakening of the old spirit, for the Prince had come, and the standard was up, and Gladsmuir had been fought, and it was "owre the border awa, awa." But he chafed in enforced seclusion away in Buchan, and thought of Sheriffmuir and Preston, for the parole he had passed at Carlisle forbade him to draw the sword again. So the old warrior sat down at home at Ludquharn, and spent hour after hour over the long declaration, that was to assure the Prince how he rejoiced at his triumph, and how he would have been with him but for the unlucky promise that had saved his head. Alas! the Prince's regard for his father's faithful follower was never put to the test of reading through that awe-inspiring document that puzzles us now, for the tide turned, and old William Forbes of Blackton laid aside the pen when he heard of Culloden. And the years rolled on, and still he lingered, and heard, perhaps, how his cousin and old comrade-in-arms, the Earl Marischall, had even in exile not forgotten Britain, but warned Lord Chatham of the Family Compact designed by the hated house of Bourbon, and how the Earl's brother had fallen "as becomes a hero" among Prussians and Austrians on the field of Hochkirchen. But at last the chair was empty, and the snuff-box no longer opened, and the shoe-buckles put reverently away, and one who loved him wrote, " our old friend, Blackton, is now I hope at his happie rest."

The Forbeses of Blackton were directly descended from the chief of their name, and old charters show that the lands of Blackton had been for some time in possession of their ancestors, the Lords Forbes. In 1581, William (7th) Lord Forbes granted a charter of Blackton to Abram Forbes, his fifth and youngest lawful son. Through his mother, Elizabeth, daughter of Sir William Keith of Inverugy, Abram Forbes was connected with the great northern house of the Earl Marischall, and marrying " Janet

Duncan, daughter to James Duncan of Meldrum (or Mardrum) and relict of the Laird of Belhe Irvine," he became the founder of the family whose story we propose, as far as may be, to reconstruct. We learn from Lumsden's "Genealogie of the Houss of Forbes" that he had a large family, "James Forbes of Blacktoune, Arthur, William and John Forbes: also he had fyve daughters; the eldest married on the laird of Finrersie in Moray; the 2nd, married on Harthill Leith; the 3rd, on John Leith of Whithaugh; the 4th, on the barrone of Braishley; the 5th married Dr. Wm. Johnstone." "As to the posteritie," adds Lumsden, "of Arthur, Wm., and John Forbess's sons to Abraham Forbes of Blackton, we know non, save one daughter, married to   Dunbar, brother to Kilbuyack."

On the 18th of August, 1604, Abraham Forbes appeared at Aberdeen as a witness to a charter by which James Ogilvy of Bleraik granted to Marjorie Gordon, daughter of George Gordon of Cocklarachie, and future spouse of James Ogilvy, son and heir-apparent of the said James Ogilvy of Blerack, "the town and lands of Eister Toune of Auchlewchres, with the Milne and Milne lands in liferent for all the days of her life." She was the grandmother of General Patrick Gordon, that famous soldier of fortune who was the right hand man of Peter the Great; who, when his own sovereign lost his crown at the battle of the Boyne, bewailed the fate that prevented him "giving proofs of my loyalty and what I can do"; and of whom his biographer remarks:—"We can well believe that the hand which crushed the Strelitzes would have been heavy upon the Cameronians."

We find Abraham Forbes, in 1606, in a transaction which speaks of troubled times and the feudal rivalry of old days. It is a "submission and Decreet Arbitrall between the clan and name of Forbes and the hous of Drum Irwine," and the Laird of Blackton appears along with the "richt honorabill Arthur Maister of Forbes, Johne Forbes of Pitsligo, William Forbes of Tochone, Johne Forbes of Brux, and James Gareauche of Kilstaris "for ourselffis and taking the burding on us conjunctlie and severallie for the haill clan and name of Forbes, ours and thairis haill kin, freindis, dependeris, tennentis, followeris, servantis, partakeris, and all utheris whom we may stope or lett directlie or indirectlie." Certain of the Forbesses and their friends had assaulted some of the Irvines and their friends, and killed one of their servants, "quhilk being clene contrarie to "our honour and lang continewit friendship with the houss of Drum, in signification of our affection to the said hous of Drum, and hatred to the said enormitis," these leading barons of the Forbes clan obliged themselves to force their fugitive clansmen to "abyd at undirly and fulfill quhatsumever decreit and sentence, it sall pleiss Alexander Irvine of Drum, be himselff alane or be quhomesoewir utheris he pleisses to pronunce and insert on the blank subscrywit on the bak heirof aganis the said fugitives." They further bound themselves and their clan not to "mantene, assist, fortifie, defend, ressait, succour, support, harbour, hous, or hald, entertene, gif counsell or releiff, or mak moyen in ony sort," to the transgressors, and that they would not "beir gruge, feid, hatred or inimitie directlie or indirectlie," against any one for "domage, hurt, or skaith," done to them, and that under a penalty. The writer of the submission was "Maister Williame Leslie of Warthill," and Alexander Burnet of Leyis was one of the witnesses.

Abraham Forbes bought, in 1607, the property of Wester-Fowlis, including Easter-Leochel and Craigmill, from Alexander Gordon of Beldornie ; but it was subsequently parted with by his grandson Walter in 1659. He must have been dead by 1637, for in that year James Forbes was retoured heir to his father, Abraham Forbes of Blackton.

Of the second Laird of Blackton, Lumsden records that he married a daughter of the Laird of Philorth, "who did bear to him Walter Forbes of Blackton, and Arthur Forbes, wt. oyr. children who bear witness themselves." He lived in troubled times, and though little is to be discovered about himself, his near relatives took part in the stirring scenes of the Civil War. Spalding introduces his account of the Trot of Turriff, the action in which the first blood was shed, with the statement that "Livetennand-Crowner Johnstoun with diverss uthers brave gentilmen about the number of 800 horss and foot, with sum good commanderis, sic as Arthur Forbes of Blacktoun quickilie brocht out of Strathbogie four feild brassin peces : and understanding the covenanteris forcess to incresse daylie, thairfour thay stoutlie resolve to tak them in tyme, and to go on with all diligens." So a representative of the Blackton branch fought well for the Cavaliers in opposition to the general tenets of his clan.

Arthur Forbes seems to have seen out "the Barons' War,' for when "the barronis upon Mononday the 20th of May rode out of Abirdene, up Diesyde to Durris, and plunderit sic as they could get from the name of Forbessis, and utheris Covenanteris. Thay war led be livetennant Crowner Johnstoun their Generall"—he "who kept the brig o' Dee"—"Crowner Gairdin, capitane Ker and Arthour Forbes of Blaktoun expert and brave commanderis who keipit their counsall of warr daylie whill as thay war in Aberdein within the tolbuith." Eight years later we find in the records of the Presbytery of Turriff, under date of 27th May, 1647, among the "names of malignants excommunicated," that of "Arthur Forbes brother to the gudeman of Blacktoun," while in those of the Synod of Aberdeen, in October 1649, we read—"It is found that Arthur Forbes of Blackton was relaxed from excommunication in Aberdeen, as also Barbara Hay, relict of umquhile Adam Straquhan."

The branch of Blacktoun, however, was also represented on the other side, for when, in 1643, Leslie's army had entered England, and the eldest son of the Marquis of Huntly was still serving with the Estates against his father, Spalding tells us, "Satterday 23rd Marche, Capitane Johne Forbes of the famelie of Blaketoun, went out of Abirdein south to the army with about 60 soldiouris under the Lord Gordon's division."

The conjuncture, however, was not a pleasant one for the Laird of Blackton, and his sympathies were evidently with his brother Arthur. The Covenanters had it all their own way at the moment, and it was the reign of the redoubtable Mr. Andrew Cant in the city of Bon-Accord. "Now thundring daylie out of pulpittes against papistis in Abirdene: none durst be sein but scirchit and socht." So says Spalding, and we learn from him that it cost the Laird of Blackton, whose family seem hitherto to have adhered to the Roman faith, their chaplain. "And upon the 18th of April, the young laird of Birkenbog (schiref of Banf) be commission, accompaneit with the ballies thereof, brocht into Abirdene ane priest called   Robertsone, who wes takein be the said schiref out of Forbes of Blacktoun's hous, and first had to Banff and straitlie wairdit, and therefra transportit to Abirdene be this schiref and ballies of Banff and brocht in to the provinciall Assemblie in New Abirdene. He wes put agane thair into the tolbuith, and schortlie thairefter transportit to Edinburgh to the counsall; and efter sum tryellis, in end he wes dismissit to Wast Flanderis, oblegit, under the paine of death, never to return back to Scotland agane."

Perhaps the activity of the sheriff of Banff, and the bailies, and those who gave them their commission, touched the little household away in the north in more ways than one, and deprived them not only of a priest but a preceptor. Their tutor gone, and taken away so forcibly, the Laird may have resolved to send his sons abroad for their education. A casual notice in "the Briefe Narration," in which Father Blackhall has preserved for posterity so interesting a picture of the perils that encountered a Jesuit confessor, and the state of the North of Scotland, from the point of view of the Roman priest, while Cavalier and Covenanter were contending for the mastery, fits in very curiously with the misfortune of Father Robertson. Worthy Father Blackhall had succeeded in getting his "third noble lady," Lady Henrietta Gordon, safely out of Scotland, and he goes on to relate:—" The ninth day of August we parted from Dieppe in a carrosse of relay, going for Rouen, for which we payed two pistoles, or twenty francks. We were sex in company in it, to wit, the ladye and her servant, the Laird of Shives, and two yong gentlemen, sonnes to Blaktoune Forbes, and me. We keeped together from Dieppe to Paris, she, her woman, and I upon her accompte, and the other three, each one for himselfe payed *pro rata*, the half of al the depense among them and we the other halfe. We arrived at Rouen that same day, where we stayed but two dayes. The twelf day we parted from Rouen in a carrosse, which we hyred only for us sex for four score francks, with obligation to go where we pleased by the way and to be three dayes betwixt Rouen and Paris. For the greater commodity of the younge ladye, the first night we lodged at Bois-dennemetz, ten ligues from Rouen, wher I was preceptor to the signeur, a yong gentleman of threttein years. We were all sex royally entertained there that night, and the ladye was over

joyed that I had brought the ladye with me out of Scotland. . . .
The second night we lay at Ponthoise, and the third at Paris, the
eve of the Assumption of Our Blessed Ladye, 1643." It is a
pleasing glimpse of what must have been a charming journey to
the "young gentlemen," finding their way to college in company
with an ecclesiastic who was also a man of the world, and the
young lady destined to become "Dame d'Attour to Madame."
What a change it must have been from bleak Banffshire, and how
they must have forgotten "the Troubles" of Great Britain, and
the "friends that were far awa'," in the warm welcome and the
royal entertainment of which the good priest retained so sweet a
recollection. The Registers of the Scots College of Douay supply
the next link, and show the purpose of the journey. In them is
entered, on 10th September, 1643, Walter Forbes, son of James
Forbes of Blacktoun and Magdalen Fraser, daughter of Sir
Alexander Fraser of Philorth. His brother, Arthur, six years
younger, and only twelve, entered on the same day. But, alas, for
the tuition of Father Robertson, and the care of Father Blackhall,
and the bright eyes of the young ladye whose carrosse he had
shared, and the training of the Scots College; for the note in its
records placed against Walter's name, is the significant one—
"*uxorem duxit, et hæreticus factus est.*"

James Forbes must have died when his son was about twenty-
two, for, in 1647, Walter Forbes was charged to enter heir to his
father, James Forbes of Blackton.

Arthur Forbes, the younger pupil of the Scots College, subsequently became Laird of Balvenie, in Banffshire. He died in
1695, and in after years the succession to Balvenie was claimed by
the last Laird of Blackton.

The brothers must also have had at least one sister, for among
the birth brieves preserved in the registers of the burgh of
Aberdeen, is one dated the 25th May, 1676, which embodies her
ancestry, and enables us to verify, and in one instance to correct,
the links in the family genealogy already referred to. "The saide
day," it runs, and it is interesting as a specimen of the class of
document, "it was judicially verified and proven, by the depositiones
of   , that Jeane Forbes, relict of the
deceast James Forbes of Bankhead, is the lauchfull daughter of

James Forbes of Blacktoun, procreat betwixt him and Magdalen Fraser his spous, in the band of lauchfull matrimonie; and that the said James Forbes of Blacktoun wes the eldest lauchfull sone and air of the deceist Abraham Forbes of Blacktoun, his father, procreat betwixt him and Janet Charters * his spous in the band of lauchfull matrimonie, who wes daughter to James Charters of Meldrum, procreat betwixt him and Janet Lumsden, lauchfull daughter to John Lumsden of Cushnie; and that the said Abraham Forbes of Blacktoune wes the lauchfull sone of William Lord Forbes, cheif of the famelie, procreat betwixt him and Dam Elizabeth Keith,   ; and the said Magdalen Fraser mother to the said Jeane Forbes is the lauchfull daughter of Sir Alexr. Fraser of Philorth, procreat betwixt him and dam Margaret Abernethie, his spous, lauchfull daughter to Alexr. Lord Abernethie of Saltoune, procreat betwixt him and dam Margaret Stewart his spous, lauchfull daughter to the Earle of Atholl; and that the said Sir Alexr. Fraser wes the lauchfull sone of Sir Alexander Fraser of Philorth, procreat betwixt him and dam Margaret Ogilvie, lauchfull daughter to the Laird of Bamff, cheife of the famelie. All quhich they deponit to be of weritie, be wertue of their great oathes sworne. Whereupon the said baillie ordanit ane testificat to be extended in ample forme, subscrivit be the clerke of the said burghe, and sealled with the secret seall of the same."

The wife whom the Douay Register associates with Walter Forbes's change of faith, was herself a Forbes of the house of Corsindae, being the third daughter of John Forbes of Balfluig, afterwards of Corsindae, by his second marriage with Elizabeth Forbes. The Records of the Presbytery of Turriff show that other and less gentle influences were also at work. Walter Forbes, it appears, bore his share in the struggles of the time; and, fighting for the king, in the last luckless effort in which Scottish Cavalier and old Covenanter alike joined, which Cromwell foiled at Preston, and which cost its leader, the Duke of Hamilton, his head, brought down upon himself the censure and the inquisitorial

---

* There is no real contradiction here, for the names of Charters and Duncan were both borne by one branch of this family.

attention of those stern ecclesiastical authorities who filled the records of the day with the witness of their zeal, in prying into private families, and prescribing the political opinions, as well as the moral conduct, of the people. The Presbytery Book of Turriff tells us that, on 31st January, 1650," Mr. William Jaffray (minister of King-Edward) reported that Walter Forbes of Blacktoun, who had been a Captain upon the last unlawful engagement, was come to the Paroche, and that without anie citatione he would compeir this day and submit himself to the censure of the Presbytery. But not compeiring according to his promiss, he is ordaned to be cited to the next day of meeting."

But the Cavalier baron must have found the prospect very distasteful, and resolved to fight it off as long as possible, for on 23rd February all the progress made is—"Walter Forbes of Blaktoun promised by letter to keep next day and submit himself to the censure of the Pby." But when next day comes, a month later (21st March), he is otherwise engaged, and "being employed in giving of a band for keeping of the peace of the country, is excused for not keeping of the pbrial meeting." He seems to have found this civil penalty of his principles sufficient for the time, without running to meet the ecclesiastical; for on the 4th April the entry is—"Walter Forbes of Blaktoun being law[lie] cited to this day and called, compeired not, he is ordained to be cited pro 2[do]."

At last on 8th May, the recalcitrant Cavalier is finally brought to book, and curiously enough it is in company with one who had been a Covenanter in the earlier phases of the struggle, and whose error in the eyes of their censors was his adhesion to the moderate party, the very sheriff who seven years before had carried off his father's confessor—" Compeared Sir Alexr. Abercrombie of Birkinboig, knicht, and confessed that he had voiced in parliament for the ingadgement, acknowledged the same in itself to be unlawfull, and his sinfullness in being accessorie yr to, supplicating that he might be received. He is ordained to subscrive the declaration and to satisfie before the congregatione of King Edward where he was to be received. Compeared also Lievetennand-Crowner Forbes, brother to Petnacaddell and Walter Forbes of Blaktoun, parochiner of King-Edward acknowledging that the late ingadgement was unlaw[ll] in itself and their own guiltiness in being accessorie yrunto, and did humbly supplicat that they might be receaved. They are ordained to subscribe the declaration, the League and the Covenant, and to satisfie before the congregation of King-Edward where they were to be received." And on 30th May the entry is:—" Sir Alexander Abercrombie of Birkinboig Lievetennant-Crowner Forbes, and Walter Forbes of Blaktoun hath satisfied as they were enjoyned." The work of conversion from Roman Catholicism to Presbyterianism seems to have taken even longer in the case of other members of the household, if the Janet Forbes of the next quotation was, as seems probable, one of the Blackton family. At the visitation of the kirk of King-Edward, on July 25th, 1650, " Compeired Janet Forbes, and professed that now at last she was brought to a knowledge of the truth of the faith of the Church of Scotland. She renounced all the poynts of Popery, and subscryved the negative confession. Ordains that she communicat with the first occasion, and that the minister publish her abjuration of Popery and subscription of the negative confession, and mak her acknowledge the same before the congregation, and so the process to ceass." And so it did cease, for on 21st August we are told " Janet Forbes hath satisfied us she wes enjoyned."

Owing to the action of his father's creditors it was not until 1654 that Walter Forbes enjoyed the full property of Blackton, and for some time the real rights had been in the hands of Lord Saltoun, from whom he fully reacquired in that year. In 1669 he disponed the fee to Alexander, his son, and in 1674 did the same with Stroquharie, which he acquired in 1673. But he was still living in 1677, when his son was still designed as younger of Blackton. He had also a daughter who, in her marriage contract, dated at Turriff, on 20th December, 1684, with John Forbes, younger, burgess of Aberdeen, is designed as Christian Forbes, daughter of the deceast Walter Forbes of Blackton. She died before 1675.

Of Walter Forbes's son, Alexander, who succeeded him as the fourth Laird of Blackton, we first discover a trace in the list of young men who, in the year 1668, entered their names on the roll of King's College, Aberdeen, "*sub regimine magistri Roberti Forbes.*" Among them is that of "Alexander Forbes, major, a

Blacktone." Little more is known of him. From a burgess ticket of Elgin, it appears that, on the 30th November, 1687, he was presented with the freedom of that town, and it is certain that in 1693 he was the husband of Isobel Hacket," relict of the deceast Alexander Abernethie of Meyan." Whether she was his first or second wife is not evident, but his eldest son, William, the last Laird was born on November 28th, 1689. He had also a daughter, Helen Forbes, who in 1712 married William Keith, younger, of Bruxie.

He disponed the fee of his estates to his son, on the occasion of his marriage in 1714, and was alive on the 19th of April, 1720, but had died in 1721.

William Forbes, his son, mentions in the long memorial, which he subsequently addressed to Prince Charles Edward, that he had served, for five or six years in Queen Anne's reign, in the army in Flanders, and had been severely wounded at the siege of Bouchain. He married on 31st August, 1714, Jane Brodie, sister of Joseph Brodie of Muiresk, and his father made over to him the fee of Blackton. His wife's obligations were undertaken with consent of "Lilias Forbes, then Lady Mountblarie, her mother," who had married, as her second husband, Andrew Hay of Mountblarie. Their union was not of long duration, for his wife had died before 1720, but they had at least one daughter, Isabella, born at Blackton, on 25th June, 1715, who married Thomas Urquhart, on 5th June, 1732.

But whatever the length of their married life, William Forbes was soon summoned away from the north, and it is almost certain that before he returned his wife was no more.

It was the year 1715.

> "The standard on the Braes of Mar
> Was up and streaming rarely,
> The gathering pipe on Lochnagar
> Was blawing loud and clearly;"

and despite the evil omen that had cast a shade over the Earl of Mar's great hunting match, most of the noblemen and gentlemen of the north, and the clansmen of many a Highland glen, had rallied to the cause of the exiled Prince. The summons to William Forbes of Blackton came, as he tells us in his Memorial, from "the Earl of Marischall, my relation"; and although his style is very diffuse and imperfect, we shall let him in the main give us the account of his own fortunes in the struggle. "The said Earl Marischal wrote from Perth to me, your Highness' Petitioner, with this present Lord Forbes, with whom I came up to Perth. I being some months before come from Flanders, a soldier there in Queen Anne's wars, and within two or three days after my arrival at Perth, I was placed Lieutenant in Captain John Gordon's company of Aboyne, who wanted an officer that had some skill in the military affairs at that very juncture of time, and I entered with half-pay till matters should be on a better footing." The Colonel of his regiment was the Earl of Panmure. He was present at the battle of Sheriffmuir, when "unluckily some on each side gave way and fled, but the most of the Duke of Argyll's men stood their ground, and took a great many prisoners, where I had the misfortune to be one. And that evening they carried us to Dunblane, where we had almost perished for cold, it being a most severe and bitter frost, had not General Wade had some compassion, and gave us fire in the open field when he heard that some of us had expired already for cold, being stripped of the most of our clothes. And the next morning they had us to Stirling Castle, where we was most barbarously used, both in the Gatehouse and the Castle. But in particular those who were put in the Gatehouse, who had not friends to speak for them to get them put in the citadel itself, and I had the bad fortune to be one of the number who was put in the Gatehouse, where we remained till the Sentries could not stand their tour without doors for the stink of the wounded and dead people"; and the prisoners suffered other hardships which it is better not to transcribe. At last, however," by the report of the sentries, those who remained alive, we were transported to Edinburgh Castle, where we lay eleven months, three weeks, and some few days, with little better usage than at Stirling. And last of all we was carried to Carlisle, where we remained nearly five months before our trial came on for Life and Death." Blackton has preserved a quaint account of the trials from the point of view of a prisoner; but it may be questioned whether he possessed in the eyes of the bench the importance he attributes to himself, though probably his experience abroad, and the little duties he seems to have discharged, made him a personage of some popularity and influence among his comrades in adversity. "And when," he continues, "King George the First's Parliament thought proper, they sent four Judges to Carlisle, to condemn or not condemn as they thought proper, upon examination of being guilty of treason (as they called it) against King George. And when the said Judges were set upon the bench of Justice, they called for the greatest and richest of the prisoners who was brought to the pannel desk before them; but, it being needless to make a detail of the whole points the Judges interrogated them upon, only, in short they pled guilty of the crime laid to their charge. The second rank being called and examined pled as the former, and both pled for mercy with the King, who, it seems, granted it, for they afterwards were pardoned and discharged. The third set being poor was called, but they thought it scarce worth their while to pass sentence upon them, so they gave them their discharges. The fourth and last rank was called, whereof there was three in number. The first, Provost Hay in Perth, who was brought to the Pannel Desk. The King's witnesses whom they had against him gave such declarations before the assizes, that he was found guilty of death, and the Judges condemned him to die and to be executed against that day fortnight; but before that day of execution, I being master-household to the prisoners by my moyen and means, I found out a way for his escape which did prove effectual. The second of the three next being called, his name and title was Stewart of Tannachie-Tulloch in the Enzie, who brought up four of his own witnesses from the Enzie, proving that he was forced and compelled by his superior, the Duke of Gordon, as so he was, to join your Royal Father's camp; and when the Judges heard his witnesses, they liberated and discharged him. And lastly, I the third being called and brought before the bar to answer conform to Law as the rest was, and I having no witnesses for me, but God's special Providence to be my support and safeguard against all their malice and envy they had against me, for they were all positively bent to bring me in Guilty of Treason to make me an example and sacrifice for all the rest of the Prisoners, seeing they had no more at all to try for Life and Death, but only I allenarly to be made a sacrifice in that respect. So my case is very lamentable to be considered on, and most bitterly and severely used every manner of way. But God's special Providence towards me was most wonderful for my deliverance for all their malice they had against me, they got not that done to make me guilty of death, for all their witnesses they had against me did all vary in their probation they pronounced against me, and so the Jury they had chosen against me before they enclosed, and I was declared not guilty of death, although they had three different Juries enclosed on me to bring me in guilty, and so they were forced and obliged to grant me a discharge for Treason against King George. The principal copy of the discharge given me by the Judges, the first part of it which I have to produce, your Royal Highness, is written in Latin with the old Chancery hand, which I do not understand, nor can write it after that form and tenor. And the second part of it in English, is as follows,—"These are humbly to certify that at the said special Commission held at Carlisle, before the Honourable the Justices Commissioners above mentioned, and appointed by His Majesty's letters patent, made according to an Act of Parliament, entituled an Act for the more easy and speedy trial of such persons as have levied or shall levy war against His Majesty; William Forbes of Blackton, in the shyre of Aberdeen, gentleman, being committed for High Treason, was discharged out of custody by proclamation in open Court.

So signed by Thomas Bretton, Clerk of Arraignments.

Discharge by the Judges, in Carlisle, to Blackton, in Dec., 1717."
And in the last place they sent all their officers for me, some few hours after I was liberated out of prison, when I was clearing accounts with the merchants in Carlisle for necessaries I had gotten for the prisoners use, I being Master-household as above said, and after search made for me, they at last found me, and these officers compelled me to return back where the King's Judges was into one Mrs. Patterson's House, Vintner there, and when I appeared again before them, they put an oath on me, after they had fenced a Court in that House for that very end, which was a sacred and heavy oath, and was obliged to swear and pronounce it with my hands on the Bible, the word of God, or else return immediately back to prison. The nature of the oath is as follows, That I should not rise or levy war against the House of Hanover, or any of the branches of it that had title right or pretension

to the Crown of Britain's Realms, for year and day after the first insurrection that should chance or happen to be in the Race on name of Stewart that had any right to the Crown of Britain," "And now," adds the old Jacobite, writing thirty years after the events he has been describing—"after that trial for life and death your Royal Highness is the first of that name that hath come to Scotland." Traced in his own hand, and on paper brown with age, his story brings vividly before us the suffering and the peril, the escape he had made, and the shock he must have received, when called again before the Judges, from whose hands he had slipped, through the good offices of successive Juries. The Jacobites of a later day were to have a different experience of English Juries, and it was well for old Blackton that that "sacred and heavy oath" prevented him tempting his fate in their hands again. It is not unlikely that he had been marked as a fit subject of example, owing to his having held the Royal Commission in the British army, and the policy of sternly discouraging the adhesion of trained soldiers to the cause of the Chevalier St. George.

More than two years must have elapsed from the time he rode away from Blackton to join the army of King James VIII. at Perth, before William Forbes, with more signs of age on him than two years would account for, found himself once more on the banks of the Deveron, and exchanged the dungeons of Carlisle for those breezes from the Northern Sea, of which a local distich, speaking of a neighbouring mansion, says—

> "Cauld blaws the wind
> Aboot the hoose o' Eden."

Five years pass from the date of the Carlisle discharge, and we find him again entering the bonds of matrimony, his second wife being, as had been the first, the daughter of a neighbouring laird. The first Lady of Blackton had been a Brodie of Muiresk, and her mother had been a Forbes; the second was a Cumine of Auchry, and her mother was a Forbes also. At Auchry, on 6th December, 1722, the marriage contract was signed between William Forbes and Mrs. Mary Cuming, daughter of John Cuming of Auchry and Anna Forbes, his present spouse. The old words of style are quaint, and after binding them to "solemnize the honourable bond of matrimony, in face of Holy Kirk, by the words of the present tyme," further oblige them "thereafter to love, cherish, intertain, and treat one another as becometh Christian married persons of their Rank and Degree." The Blackton Estate is described as "all and haill the touns and lands of Blacktoun, Badentoy, and Watcriestacks, and the Milne of Blacktoun, Milne lands, multers sucken, sequels, and knaveships thereof, with the Manor place of Blackton, houses, biggings, yards, Tofts, crofts, mosses, muirs, annexes, connexes, parts, pendicles, and pertinents of the said haill lands lying within the parishon of King Edward and Sheriffdom of Aberdeen," and along with it were disponed to Blackton and his spouse in conjunct fee and liferent, "all and haill the Touns and Lands of Straquharie." As the destination ran to the heirs male of the marriage, whom failing, to the heirs male of the body of William Forbes by any other marriage, whom failing, to his nearest heirs and assignees "quhatsomever," it is evident that he had no son by his former marriage.

But the connection of the Forbeses with Blackton was now near its close, and that estate experienced the common fate of the properties of the smaller Jacobite Lairds of Banffshire. On 2nd December, 1725, it was parted with to William Duff of Braco.

Of the future fortunes of its former owner there is little to be said. He had, in 1727, a tack of Pittrichie, and afterwards lived for some time in the neighbourhood of his relatives, the Keiths of Bruxie, at Brownhill of Altrie, at Skelmuir, and at Ludquharn, all of them places in the neighbourhood of Old Deer. At one time the opening of a succession to his grand-uncle, Arthur Forbes of Balveny, gave promise of retrieving the fortunes of their house; but Balveny had been heavily burdened, and the creditors' rights had been acquired by Duff of Braco, now raised to the peerage of Ireland as Lord Braco, and in the lawsuit that ensued he succeeded in maintaining the possession he had obtained.

William Forbes was living at Ludquharn when Prince Charles Edward landed in Lochaber, and the rising of 1745 took place. The story we have quoted of his experiences in the '15, is taken from two long Memorials which he composed in the stirring times of the '45, to justify himself to the Prince for not having rallied at once to his standard. The first, addressed to "The most noble Prince Charles, Regentte of Brittanse Realmes," is dated 31st October, 1745, and the second, February 22nd, 1746. Both cover much the same ground, though the second is more complete in its narrative and better expressed, and the purpose of both is to state "two very great impediments and reasons standing in my way why I could not get joined to the rest of the Gentlemen and others of Inferior ranks with them even at your Highness first entry into Scotland in the Highlands and since that time."

The first of these impediments was the oath which he had been compelled to take at Carlisle, and he points out that a similar oath had been administered by the Prince to an officer taken prisoner near Fort-William, and to those taken at Gladsmuir. "And some hath obeyed and some hath not." "Now in my weak opinion," he reasons, "this oath I made was somewhat sacred, although it was authorized by old authority they had it from in some measure. So its one reason which did detain my not obeying your highness order to repair to the standard ye had set up for all well-hearted and wishing subjects to the true line, to repair to the standard aforesaid." And referring to the case of Captain Swinton at Fort-William, " reported hereabout in this corner where I reside at," he guards the reference thus—" But I might own and acknowledge it, your oath, tendered to him has far more strength in it, it being tendered to him from the true spring and fountain head of the race that has the best right to the Crown of Britain, &c. So as your character of clemency, mercy and forgiveness to all your enemies doth extend as far as it doth, I am hopeful and do plead for the same benefit at your hands in this my case and circumstances, if it can consist with your Grandeur and privilege to do in that respect." "In my weak opinion," he says again in the second Memorial, vindicating himself from "not appearing at your Royal standard as other true Loyalists have done," "any person whatsomever that would violate such an oath cannot be pardoned but by the great Judge of Heaven and Earth; and although the oath was unlawfully imposed by the King's Judges, yet their authority there was strong and violent against those of my circumstances at that time. So when the time is fully expired, through God's assistance nothing shall oppose my joining wherever your Royal standard shall be set up, if health and strength remain to me." He refers to the 5th and 6th verses of the 27th chapter of the Book of Job,* as apposite "to my case and downright integrity of heart," and adds—"providing I would have been contented to have been a knave, or to be a witness against the rest of the prisoners with me, I would have gotten gold and monies offered me in plenty, but that I disdained to take in any respect."

The second impediment was of a more permanent nature, being the great law-plea about Balveny, in which, doubtless, old Blackton was not swayed to take a more friendly view of his opponent, by the fact that he was also the new possessor of his own paternal estate. Some of the pleadings are signed by Duncan Forbes, and the stake was a rental of £3000 sterling a year. It was quite an old-fashioned lawsuit, of the good old Scots heritable right kind that went on for years; that "process commenced in December, 1733, with one Duff Lord Braco, my antagonist, for the lands and lordship of Balvenie Estate, which belonged heritably to my Grand-uncle, Arthur Forbes, Proprietor of that large Estate, who had no issue of his own body at all, but fell in to me by blood, being nearest of kin to him." Of "Lord Braco, as he is called and termed at present by the whole vulgar in the country," Blackton sarcastically observes, "but that title and name he has acquired till now-a-days is gotten by his weighty purse, but not by his valour and other qualifications of his own merit." His feelings towards "my sore antagonist,"† were more embittered by the recollection of previous relations of friendship and obligation that had existed between Arthur Forbes of Balvenie and Alexander Duff of Braco, the uncle of the "antagonist." His sentiments towards the civil judges of Scotland were not more friendly than to the commission that had dispensed English Criminal Law at Carlisle. Indeed, he asserts that one of the Scots Bench had been got at by

---

* "God forbid that I should justify you : till I die I will not remove mine integrity from me.

"My righteousness I hold fast, and will not let it go : my heart shall not reproach me so long as I live."

† The opponent's repute as a litigious neighbour and a "sore antagonist" was such that it is said to have "made John, Earl of Kintore, add a new petition to his prayers, 'Lord, keep the hill o' Foudlin between me and Braco.'"

his opponent, and made to act as a "decoy-duck" to his brethren on the Bench. But there is faith in the old Jacobite that

"All will go well
When the king enjoys his own again;"

and after more than ten years of expensive and fruitless litigation, he is content "to wait patiently" till things are in a better condition, "for my good profit and advantage in getting this affair and law-plea of mine fairly debated and pled before the honourable bench of Lords of Session at Edinburgh, when your Majesty or Highness shall think proper to place just judges on the bench of Justice." Such, however, had been the effect of the luxury of litigation and the swoop of creditors that followed upon an adverse judgment, that he describes himself as not having the wherewithal "to buy for myself or family with me boll or half-boll or firlot of any sort of meal." "Upon honour and word of a gentleman and honest man as God is my witness at present, and as long days hence do pass he will be my judge on it, I am writing or saying nothing but verity and truth." There is something very plaintive in the petition of the unfortunate "gentleman and honest man," to the "generosity, candour, and great clemency" of the Prince, "in this my case and condition I am presently situate intill." "I do most earnestly plead," writes Blackton, "you will forgive my not joining in coming up with the rest of your subjects that's just now with you in that camp near by Holyrood House, your noble policy there."

"And now," he says, in spite of the impediments that prevent greater efforts, "in the last of this long petition and information writ your Royal Highness P.R. I will risk all hazards in a safe conscience joining along with it, If I can be capable or able to do it in any measure whatsoever in this corner of the countrie I do live and reside intil. I should do my best endeavour I can or could do for to raise men for your service providing I had money sent me to do it." "I know," he explains, "the way and means of engaging and taking on soldiers for such service as your service would be, I being a soldier myself in Flanders." But after mentioning his experience there, there comes a doubt—"If I have not forgotten the exercises of the military manner," or the exercise he knew were out of date. Yet, "with the most frank offer and service I am capable to undertake or do in your valuable noble service," with an assurance of the "utmost earnestness, anxiety, and desire for to obey and revere your noble Highness' orders and commands," he signs himself "most respectfully while I live and breathe, Most Noble Prince Charles Regent, your Royal Highness's most sincere wellwisher to Power, William Forbes."

But sincere wishes in Buchan were of little avail against divided counsels at Derby, and it must have been a dark and bitter day at Ludquharn, when there travelled there the tale of Culloden. The vision of a reformed Court of Session, the hope of any reward in the future for the sufferings of the past had vanished, and the Memorials were put sadly and silently away. And we hear little further of Blackton, though he lived thirty years longer. Whether he had more vicissitudes, when Gordon of Glenbucket's Highlanders roved through the Laigh of Buchan, to be succeeded by the redcoated musketeers of Cumberland, and the clansmen of Argyle who wore the black cockade, and gave to the flames the neighbouring chapels of Old Deer and Longside, we cannot tell.

His second wife had died before 1763,* and in 1756 he had seen his grand-daughter, Elizabeth Urquhart—described, twelve years later, by the *Aberdeen Journal*, in the quaint manner of the time, as " in every relation of life an example of those virtues which render the female sex truly amiable"—follow the fashion of her generation, by making a runaway marriage with the only son of their neighbour, Kinmundy. At last, about three o'clock in the morning of 9th Octobey, 1771, the last Forbes of Blackton ceased to live, and the end was intimated in words of quiet pathos, as the reaching of " his happy rest."

Such are the fragmentary notices which enable us to gather the skeleton of a narrative that illustrates very well the story of a typical family of the north of Scotland. It was from such such houses that the Cavaliers drew the substance of their strength; it was men of like stamp that rallied most loyally around the

---

*From a letter, dated August 20th, 1752, in which Mr. Cumine of Auchry speaks of " Bruxie's son being left heir and executor by Testament to your son," it appears that William Forbes had a son who had by that time predeceased him.

standard of the Young Chevalier. Families like that of Blackton swelled the dark lists of condemnation and forfeiture after Culloden. But the Blackton history has its points of contrast. We should not have looked for that precise type in the "clan and name of Forbes." While it exhibits the full strength of the Scottish sentiment of kinship and clanship, and we recognise the clansman and the feudal baron of the Lowlands merging into each other across the indistinct and indefinite line that separates them, we see that sentiment yielding to the principles and passions of civil strife. But to those who can read a little below the lines the simple references strung together tell of national character and local colouring, of a native Romanist element in a Protestant country, holding the remnant of its ground with tenacity, of the old life of the Scottish gentleman, and of the heroic chivalry with which he dared all for a perilous cause and an ancient line to which his English compeer was content to drink.

ARM CHAIR OF WILLIAM FORBES.

APPENDIX.

APPENDIX.

I.

The Position of the Scots Brigade in Holland.

"ALTHOUGH the Scots Brigade were not in the pay of their own country until the year 1688, yet they had subsisted more than a century before by the authority of the Crown of Scotland, and were permanent on the Peace Establishment of that kingdom at the time they were sent last to the defence of the United Netherlands, since which time the order of the Sovereign by which they were employed abroad, remained in force until the year 1782."—*Preface to Historical Account of the Scots Brigade, 1795.*

The three English Dutch regiments that came over with King William, have ever since been on the establishment, and are now the 5th and 6th of the British line.

The three Scotch "came upon the establishment at the same time with the 5th and 6th."—*Historical Account, p. 1.*

"The question of rank seems to have been decided betwixt the English and Scotch by the antiquity of the regiments; but as royal troops both always ranked before the troops of the United Provinces, or those belonging to German Princes, which right never was contested with regard to the Scots Brigade, until the year 1783."—*Historical Account, p. 25.*

1678. Capitulation fixing footing of British Regiments in Holland.

"Officers of the Brigade serving in Holland took rank in Britain according to the date of their commissions, in whatever language they were written."—*Historical Account, p. 58.*

"While the British regiments were in the pay of Holland the officers' commissions were in the name of the States, and it was not thought necessary they should have other commissions, even when they were upon the establishment of their own country, until vacancies happened, in which case the new commissions were in the king's name. Thus when Colonel H. Mackay came over to England on the recall of the Brigade in 1685, King James promoted him to the rank of Major-General, not considering him the less as a Colonel in his army that his former commission was in the name of the States. And when the same General Mackay, who held his regiment by a Dutch commission, was killed, the regiment was given a few days after to Colonel Aeneas Mackay, whose commission is English and in the name of King William and Queen Mary."—*Historical Account, p. 69.*

This is confirmed by General Ferguson's commissions. The earlier ones, prior to the Revolution, are all in Dutch and run in the name of the Stadtholder and the States. Unfortunately his commission as Major, the only one given when the Scots Brigade proper was serving on the British establishment, is not existent. It would have been interesting to have found it running in English. His Lieutenant-Colonel's commission is not so valuable as an illustration of the Scots Brigade, because of his transfer to a new regiment raised in Scotland. But, as it is, it agrees with Colonel Mackay's and runs in the usual British form. And when the Cameronians were actually on the Dutch establishment for a short period, his commission of 1698 (as captain) bears testimony to their anomalous position. It runs in Dutch, is granted by "His Majesty" at Kensington, but enregistered by the Dutch Council of State and the States of Zealand.

"At the Peace of Ryswick in 1697, the Scots Brigade, returning to Britain with the rest of the army, was mostly stationed in Scotland, being on the establishment of that kingdom; though we find that some Scotch regiments were then on the English establishment, such as the Earl of Orkney's regiment, known now by the name of the Royal, which consisted of twenty-six companies. The total of the troops on the English establishment in the year 1698, after the Dutch Guards and all the foreign troops had been dismissed, amounted only to seven thousand men : that being the number to which the land forces were restricted by Parliament, besides those on the Irish establishment ; so that the reduction must have been very great, for immediately after the Peace of Ryswick the number of the troops on the English establishment alone amounted to 20,943, besides the foreign troops then in English pay. If the troops of Scotland were reduced in the same proportion, the three regiments distinguished by the name of the Scots Brigade, must have made a very considerable part of the peace establishment of that kingdom. It appears that there was no intention of these regiments being again in the pay of the Dutch Republic, otherwise it is natural to suppose they would have been left in the Netherlands when the rest of the British troops came over at the Peace of Ryswick, or that they would have been sent to Holland in 1698, when the great reduction took place."

The extracts from the Dutch records quoted in the text and notes prove that this passage is erroneous. They show that Lauder's and Colyear's regiments, which appears to have been in Holland in 1690, and another, probably Murray's, being the three old Scots regiments, did remain in Holland in 1697 ; and the place of the three English Regiments that came over with the Prince had been temporarily supplied by three new Scottish regiments, including the Cameronians. In 1698 Hamilton's was recalled to Scotland, and in 1699 Ferguson's and Lord Strathnaver's. They probably were the regiments referred to as sent again to Holland in 1701, for the *Historical Account*, after mentioning the Dutch political co-operation with the King's policy at that time, continues—"His

Majesty in return did all that lay in his power to assist them ; for which end he sent the three Scottish regiments retained in his own pay over into Holland. The States General in their instructions to their ambassador in England to thank the King, upon that occasion, make no mention of those regiments as having been formerly in their pay, but call them in general terms—three Scotch regiments, two of ten companies each, and one of eight ; and instruct the ambassadors to request that the regiment of eight companies may be completed by drafts from the other Scotch regiments." . . . "During the war of the Succession three new raised Scotch regiments were added to the brigade, and the whole commanded by John, Duke of Argyll, whose commission as Brigadier was from the States General."—*Historical Account, p. 76.*

These new regiments were reduced in Holland in 1710, and in consequence of a financial dispute between Great Britain and Holland, £64,000 was granted by Parliament for payment of their arrears.

"In the year 1782, it was resolved by the States General that an edict should be issued obliging the officers of the Scotch Brigade to declare that they acknowledged no Power but them as their lawful Sovereign ; that his Majesty's Royal Colours, which had come off triumphant from so many battles and sieges, should be taken from them, and that the British uniform, sash and gorget, beat of drum, and word of command should be abolished, and the regiments totally changed into Dutch troops."—*Historical Account, p. 90.*

The officers had hitherto (at least from 1757) taken the same oath of allegiance to the British Crown as those of other regiments. The Prince of Orange in his letter, of December, 1782, to the brigade, specially commanded that the uniforms should be made blue instead of red, and that orange sashes should be provided.

Some notes on the Scots Brigade were published in 1774, under the title of " Strictures of military discipline, in a series of letters, with a military discourse, in which is interspersed some account of the Scotch Brigade in the Dutch service, by an officer." Speaking of the position of the British, as compared with the Swiss in the Dutch service, the writer says,—" They enjoy no privilege as British troops, except the trifling distinction of being dressed in red, taking the right of the army when encamped or on a march, and having twopence a week more pay for the private men than the Dutch troops have."—See also Article on " The Scots Brigade " in the " Scottish Review " No. 6, April, 1884.

II.

Commissions in the Scots Brigade.

1. *Commisson as Vendrig or Ensign.*

ALSOO de vendrigh's plaetse van de compagnie van den Capitain van Zuijlen Zijnde komen te vaceren noodigh is dat de selve met een ander bequaem person werde versien ;

Soo ist dat Sijne Hoogheijt daer toe gestelt en gecommitteert heest, stelt en committeert mits desen James Ferguson
Lastende d'officieren en gemeene Soldaten van de selve compagnie den voor-noemden james ferguson voor haeren vendrigh te houden en t'erkennen—gedaen in's Hage   den 9 September, 1678.
        (Signed)   G. Prince d'Orange.
                        Ter Orde. van S. Hoogh^t
                        J. C. Huijgens.

This commission is endorsed in name of the States of Zealand.

2. The first commission, of 22nd March, 1688, as Captain, contains the additional clause:—

"Ende versoekende de Ed. Mo. Heeren, Raden van State hem met behoorlycke commissie te willen doen versien."

This commission is not endorsed, as most of the others are, on behalf of the States of Zealand, but the records in the Rijks Archief at the Hague contain this reference.

"1. April, 1688. Commissie als Capiteyn voor Jacob Ferguson in plaats van den Capiteyn George Hamilton op Holland.

which evidently relates to the following—

3. Commission as Captain, 1 April, 1688.

De Staten Generael der Vereenichde Nederlanden. Allen den geenen die desen sullen sien Salugt. Alsoo de Compagnie van den Capitein George Hamilton sijnde comen te vaceren noodigh is, dat deselve wederom met een ander bequaem ende Crijgs erwaren persoen werde voorsien Doen te weeten dat wij ons betrouwende op de kloeikhejt ende erwarensheijt uit stuck van de Oorloge van den Lieutenant Jacob Ferguson hebbe denselven bij deliberatie van den Rade van State der voorse Vereenighde Landen gestelt ende gecommitteert, stellen ende committeren bij dese tot Capitein over de voorse comp^e tot alsuliken getalle als geordonneert is off noch geordonneert sal worden, gewapent ende getracteert volgens de Lijste ende ordonnantie van 'S Landswegen alreede gemaekt off noch te maecken. Gevende hem volcomen last, macht ende bevel over deselve Comp^e te gebreden, die te geleijden ende te gebrieijken tegens de Vijanden deser Vereenighde Nederlanden t' sij te velde ofte in guarinsoen tot bewaernisse van eenige steden ofte Sterikten, oock op den Schepen van oorloge des noot sijnde daer ende soot hem bij ons oft bij den geenen van ons last hebbende tot den voorse Landen dienst sal worden geordonneert ende bevoolen, houdende bij Capitein sijne soldatene in goede ordre, wacht, ende Criggs disciplinne, soo bij dage als bij nachte, souder te gedoogen dat sij de Bergere ende Ingesetene van de Steden ende platten Lande eenige Schade ofte overlast aen doen, ende voorts alles te doen dat een goet ende getrouw Capitein schuldigh is ende behoort te doen, achter volgende de Crijgs Ordonnantie ende artijikels Brieff, opt belegt vom der oorloge gemaeckt oft noch te maken, ende dit op de Gagie in de voorse Lyste gespecificeert, ter maent tot twee en veertigh Dagen gerekent, daerop hij sijne Bevel hebberen ende soldaten Ons ende de voorse Landen getrouwelt sullen dienen souder eenigh weder seggen ende hun (?) oock seliken des vermaent sijnde on-weijgere laten monsteren des voort den voorm Ferguson gehouden van hem hierinne welende getrouwelt te quiten te doen den behoorte Eedt in hande van den gem^e Rade van State, ende dese sijne Commissie te doen registeren soo wel in de Secretarie van den selven Rade als bij de Heeren Staten van Holland ende Westvriesland op wiens Repartitie bij sal betaelt werden, daertoe hem oock behoor-lycke brieven van attache van den Heer Gouverneur ende Gecommitteerde Raden van denselven Lande sal werden verleem welck gedaen sijnde lasten ende ordonneren Wij den Lieutenant Bevelhebberen ende gemeene Soldates ende allen diene aengere mach den voorn Jacob Ferguson voor onsen bestelden Cap^n· te kennen hem te gehoorsaemen ende obedieren oock des noot en versocht sijnde alle be hulpende addres te doen ende dit alles tot Onse weder segge wenn wij sulx tot dienste van Lande bevoenden hebben te behooren. Gegeven ins Graven Hage den eersten April xvjc. acht en achtigh.

       (Signed) P. R. Zoete de Laeke Van Villets."
Regter. Fol. 157

This is endorsed—
" Ter Ordonnane van Ho. Mo. Heeren Staten Generael
 der Vereeniehde Nederlanden.
Ter Relatie van den Rade van State derselven Landen.
  (Signed) G. Van Slingelandt."

On another fold it is also endorsed—
"Jacob Ferguson heest op dese Commissie als Capitein
 gedaen den behoerlijcken Eede van getreuwigh in
 handen van de Ed. Mo. Heeren Raden van State
 der Vereenighde Nederlanden den eersten April 1688.
  My present,
  (Signed) G. Van Slingelandt."

A separate piece of parchment, attached by a seal and written in a different hand, is in these terms :—

" Sijnne Hoogheijt Wilhem Henrik bij der Gratien Godes Prince van Orange ende van Nassau, Grave van Catzenellenbogen, Wianden, Diets (?), Buijren, Leerdam, en Marquis van den Meere ende van Vlissingen, Heere ende Baron van Breda der Stadt Grave, ende den Lande van Ouijck, Hiest (?) Grimbergen, Herstal, Oranendonck, Warneston, Arlaij, Roseroij, St. Wiit, Haelburgh (?), Polanen, Willemstadt, Rierwaert, ijsselsteijn, St. Maartensdijck, Steenbergen, Gertruijdenberg, en de hooge ende de lage Zwaluwe, Raaltwijck, en Duffburgh-grave van Antwerpen, ende Besancon, Duffmaarschalk van Hollandt, Duff-stadthouder ende Gouverneur van Hollandt Zeelandt ende Westvrieslandt. Capiteijn Generael ende Admirael der Vereeniehde

Nederlanden, Mittgader de Gecommitteerde Raden van de Staten van Hollandt ende Westvrieslandt. Doen te weeten dat wij gesien ende gevisiteert hebben de geannixeerde Commissie de selve houden voorge-uitermeert, ende dat wij over sulx die in onse registre hebben doen registeren soo dat in conformite van dien aan Jacob Ferguson, eensamentlijck sijnde ouder hebbende Bevel hebberne ende soldaten de betalinge als in de selve Commissie bij ons versoreht worden naar behooren. Mits dat den voorn Capiteijn aan-nemen sal t' gemeene Landt te voldoen vant gene den affgegaen Capiteijn aant Landt soude mogen schuldigh welen ende Zij van verschot van freminge bevoringe van wapenen vivres, ouder-hout van krane de soldaten off anders. Gelijck den selven Capiteijn mede aanden affgegaen Capiteijn sal moet en betalen alle t' gene den selven sal komen bewijlen aan de Compagnie ten achteren te welen, t' Zij van Leeimige kliedinge wapenen rant, Zoenement ofte anders tot ouder-hout van de selve verstreckt. Alles op freijne dat wij desen houden voor met geintermeert ofte geadmitteert nochte in de betalinge geconsenteert. Gedaen in den Hage ondert cleijne Segel van den Lande de ii. Aprill xvi. acht en achtigh.

Regt. die Sinantie van Hollant Fol. 158.

Ter Ordonnantie van Sijnne Hoogheijt ende de Gecommitteerde Raden.

(Signed)   Simon van Beaumont.

Op-huij-den de ii. April, 1688, heest den Capitein.
Jacob Ferguson op dese Commissie gedaen die
behoorlijcke eede van suijveringe.

Mij present,
(Signed)   Simon van Beaumont.

4. *Commission as Captain in the Cameronian Regiment.*

" Sijne Majesteijt, heest gestelt ende gecommitteert stelt ende committeert mits deesen tot Capiteyn over een Compagnie te voet den Collonel James Ferguson,
Lastende d'officieren ende geemene soldaten van de selve compagnie den voorn James Ferguson voor haeren Capiteyn te houden ende te erkennen.
Ende versoekende de Ed. Mo. Heeren Raeden van Staeten hem met behoorlycke commissie te willen voorsien. Gedaen op kensington den 1en January, 1698.

(Signed)   William R.
Ter ordie. van Sijne Majt.
by absentie van den Secretaris
(Signed)   S. van Huls.

This Commission is also endorsed on behalf of the States of Zealand. The seal on the face bears the British arms, with the lion of the House of Nassau in an inescutcheon of pretence. The stamp on the back shows the demi-lion rising from the waves of Zealand.

III.

The following is the proclamation issued after Drummondernoch's murder :—

"*Edinburgh, 4th February, 1589.*

"The same day, the Lords of Secret Council being crediblie informed of ye cruel and mischeivous proceeding of ye wicked Clangrigor, so lang continueing in blood, slaughters, herships, manifest reifts, and slouths committed upon his Hieness' peaceable and good subjects : inhabiting ye countries ewest ye brays of ye Highlands, thir money years bygone ; but specially heir after ye cruel murder of umqll Jo. Drummond of Drummoneyryuch, his Majesties proper tennant, and ane of his fosters of Glenartney, committed upon ye   day of last bypast, be certain of ye said clan, be ye council and determination of ye haill, avow and to defend ye authors yrof quoever wald persew for revenge of ye same, qll ye said Jo. was occupied in seeking of venison to his Hieness, at command of Pat. Lord Drummond, stewart of Stratharne, and principal forrester of Glenartney ; the Queen, his Majesties dearest spouse, being yn shortlie looked for to arrive in this realm. Likeas, after ye murder committed, ye authors yrof cutted off ye said umqll Jo. Drummond's head, and carried the same to the Laird of M'Grigor, who, and the haill surname of M'Grigors, purposely conveined upon the Sunday yrafter, at the Kirk of Buchquhidder ; qr they caused the said umqll John's head to be pnted to ym, and yr avowing ye sd murder to have been committed by yr communion, council, and determination, laid yr hands upon the pow, and in eithnik, and barbarous manner, swear to defend ye authors of ye sd murder, in maist proud contempt of our sovrn Lord and his authoritie, and in evil example to others wicked limmaris to do ye like, give ys sall be suffered to remain unpunished."

Then follows a commission to the Earls of Huntly, Argyle, Athole, Montrose, Pat. Lord Drummond, Ja. Commendator of Incheffray, And. Campbel of Lochinnel, Duncan Campbel of Ardkinglas, Lauchlane M'Intosh of Dunnauchtane, Sir Jo. Murray of Tullibarden, knt., Geo. Buchanan of that Ilk, and And. M'Farlane of Ariquocher, to search for and apprehend Alaster M'Grigor of Glenstre, (and a number of others nominatim), "and all others of the said Clangrigor, or ye assistars, culpable of the said odious murther, or of thift, reset of thift, herships, and sornings, qrever they may be apprehended. And if they refuse to be taken, or flees to stiengths and houses, to pursue and assege them with fire and sword ; and this commission to endure for the space of three years."

In his genealogy of the Drummonds (written in 1681), Lord Strathallan says that Thomas, the 4th son of Malcolm of Cargill, was the first Laird of Drummond-Irenoch. " In his time that unlucky action of burning the kirk of Monyvaird fell out ; after which, he being in the castle of Drummond in company with his nephew, David Drummond, second son to John Lord Drummond and brother to Malcolm, then master of Drummond, the hous was rendered to King James the Fourth ; but this Thomas Drummond refusing to give himselfe up with the rest upon such insecure terms (fearing what happened soone after), leaped over the castle wall, and so escaped into the wood close beside the hous, and was, for that and some other bold pranks, called "Tom unsained." He fled first to Ireland, thereafter to London, where he procured favour from King Henrie the Seventh of England; by whose mediation and intercession he got a pardon from King James IV." The lands he subsequently acquired bore testimony to his exile, the name being changed from Waigtoune to Drummond-Irenoch, "which signifies the Irish Drummonds' lands." His grandson was the father of John Drummond of Drummond-Irenoch, "killed by the clangreigors anno 1589," and also of David Drummond, "who, for his quantity, was called 'Mikel Davie'," the first Laird of Invermay. "Mr. James Drummond," says Lord Strathallan, "second son to David Drummond, first Laird of Invermay, was the first of Cultmalindie. He married Elizabeth Stuart, daughter to Mr. Harie Stuart brother to Sir Thomas Stuart of Garntullie; she had to him two sons—David, who succeeded, and John Drummonds; and three daughters—Jean, Anna, and Helen Drummonds. 2. David Drummond, now of Cultmalindie, the son of Mr. James, yet a minor, but very hopeful." The "unlucky action" of the Kirk of Monyvaird is the occasion on which the Murrays, finding the Drummonds too strong for them, shut themselves up in the church. Incensed by a shot fired from it, the Drummonds attacked and burnt the Church over their heads. It is said that "Tom unsained," whose mother was a Murray of Tullibardine, then saved the life of one of the Murrays, to whose good offices he afterwards owed his escape from Drummond Castle.

IV.

The poem forwarded by Colonel Ferguson to Principal Carstares was as follows:—

Fab. 2.   Lib. 1.   Phaedri Metaphrasis.

Ranarum proceres, paludis hujus
Et prati indigenae palude cincti !
Nonne audistis avos patresque vestros
Securos potuisse stagna circum
Exultare sua et venusta prata ?
Rex Ilignus iis dabat beatam
Vitam atque otia non periculosa.
Tunc quae me puerum puella Rana
Castis, Jupiter, osculata labris,
Quot dein rettulit osculationes,
Et cura vacuas metuque tristi !
Quot nunc millia vidimus profecta
Ad ripae ulterioris inquilinos !
Quos illic veteres novosque lusus
Una lusimus advenae hospitesque,
A Sole exoriente ad occidendum !

Sed Ranae fuimus ; fuit paludis
Ingens gloria, lausque clara prati.
Ah ! Sors nulla diu potest placere
Ventoso populo ! Sed ipsa tandem
Libertas gravis, et graves penates,
At Saturnia displiceret Ilex,
Quae prati indigenis palude cincti
Ranis otia fecerat beata.
Irato Jove, coelitumque coetu,
Optatur novus inquies-que rector,
Rectorque eligitur Ciconiarum,
Quarum exercitus ales haec pererrat,
Haec impune pererrat atque vexat
Ranarum patria ac avita stagna ;
Nec nos visere nunc licet cohortes
Ranarum per amoeniora fusas
Pratorum aequora, et invidenda regna.
Obscoenae volucres, malaeque pestes
Stagni ! nonne sat est vorasse gentem
Nobis sanguine, moribusque junctam,
Nullae at jam superent in Insula illa
Ranae legibus atque rege junctae ?
At vos, o proceres, ducesque nostri,
Clari militiae, domique clari !
Si stirpem veterem, incolamque prati,
Servatam cupitis palude cincti,
Haec gratis animis labrisque castis,
Mecum ter memorate verba loeti ;
Et nulla audeat hic natare Rana
Quae non haec memoret ter ipsa verba :
   Ilicis sacrae geniale numen !
   Quippe te priscae coluere Ranae
   Ianiis, si nos vetus arbor audis,
       Annue votis
   Quae tuas ales peregrina Ranas
   Certat infesto violare vestro,
   Sedibus nostris abigatur omnis
       Trans mare magnum.
Nos, tua nobis ope restitutae,
Ilicis circum saliemus aram,
Principis laudes celebrare gratae
       Praticolarum.

V.

The following appeared in "Northern Notes and Queries" for December, 1886, in response to enquiries on the subject of old linen :—

40. OLD LINEN (No. 29).—I believe that linen of about the year 1700 is not at all uncommon in Scottish houses, and that some exists bearing witness to the Jacobite opinions of its early owners. There is at present in the Edinburgh Exhibition a little tablecloth, one of a set which has been in Scottish hands at least since 1705. This linen has always been called the "the Dutch linen," and vague tradition says that it was presented to one of Marlborough's generals by a foreign Court. It would seem to have been woven in commemoration of the victories of the Imperialists over the Turks in the campaigns on the Danube towards the close of the seventeenth century, in which Prince Eugene took part; and there was certainly a great interchange of courtesies between the Austrians under Eugene and the British under Marlborough, after Blenheim had saved the Empire. The smaller pieces of the set have a border consisting of alternate trophies of crossed guns, crossed pikes, flags, drums, etc., and in the corners are shields with the two-headed eagle. The same arms occupy the centre of the cloth; above are representations of foot-soldiers, and below of horsemen, while lower still is depicted a town and a river running through it, and the word "Buda" woven into the cloth. "Pest," "Gran,' " Nie " are also represented, and the rest of the cloth is filled with cannon, and on either side of the centre shield flying boys blowing trumpets, and carrying branches of laurel in the other hand. The larger pieces show the same pattern repeated, and the Danube flowing along the whole length of the cloth, with Buda and Pest alternately on the north and south of the river. This linen was brought home by Major-General Ferguson of Balmakelly, who "led up the first line of foot" at the Schellenberg, and commanded one of the brigades that assaulted the village of Blenheim. It now belongs to his descendant, Mr. Ferguson of Kinmundy, Aberdeenshire. J. F.

October, 13th, 1886.

VI.

Losses of Ferguson's brigade at Schellenberg and Blenheim.

At *Schellenberg* the Guards had 4 officers, 7 sergeants, and 75 sentinels killed; 8 officers, 8 sergeants, and 127 rank and file wounded.

"Of the Earl of Orkney's first battalion of Scotch Royal" (probably the one in this brigade), there were 3 officers, 1 sergeant, and 38 rank and file killed; 10 officers, 3 sergeants, and 103 privates wounded.

[The second battalion had 2 officers, 1 sergeant, and 76 men killed: 15 officers, 12 sergeants, and 184 men wounded.]

Lieutenant-General Ingoldsby's Regiment (the Welsh Fusilier's) had 5 officers, 6 sergeants, and 60 men killed, 11 officers, 6 sergeants, and 156 men wounded.

At *Blenheim*, the guards lost the Colonel commanding, killed, and had 5 officers wounded.

Lord Orkney's two battalions had 3 officers killed, and 8 wounded.

Ingoldsby's had 9 officers wounded.

Lediard, from whom these figures are taken, does not record the losses in rank and file at Blenheim.

A French General, writing to M. Chamillard, the Secretary of State, described the second attack on Blenheim, as delivered just after Marechal Tallard had made one of his visits to the village, "redoubling his care to secure that post." "They advanced," he wrote, "to the very muzzles of our muskets, but were repulsed."

VII.

Affair of King's Mountain.

7th October, 1780.

CARTEL OF CAPT. ABRAHAM DE PEYSTER.

("The Morning Herald and Daily Advertiser," Thursday, February 14, 1782.)

Extract of a Letter to the Printer of the "Royal American Gazette."

"You will oblige me by publishing in your paper the following declaration, which, however disgraceful it is to me as a military man to appear in newspaper publications, I am induced to make, on reading a very imperfect and erroneous account of the action of the 7th of October, 1780, near *King's Mountain*, as inserted in the *Political Magazine* of February last, p. 60; and in which my conduct is most falsely and injuriously misrepresented.

"The approbation with which my conduct has been honored by Colonel BALFOUR, the Commandant of *Charlestown*, and the voluntary testimony of Lieutenant ALLAIRE, as published in *Messrs. Well's Gazette* of the 4th of August last [1781], (and which you are desired to reprint with this), who was an eye-witness to the whole of my behaviour in the transactions of that unsuccessful day, but which became so only from the *vast inferiority of the number of Royal Troops* under my late gallant friend and commanding officer *Lieutenant-Colonel* FERGUSON, to that of the Rebels, will, I trust, be sufficient evidence for the candid and unbiassed to discredit that infamous falsehood with which my character has been basely traduced, and scandalously aspersed, by some dark and designing villain, whom I thus publicly call upon to disavow in the same public manner the account he has given of my conduct; or by announcing himself as the author, give me an opportunity of convincing him personally, and thereby the world, that whenever my own honor or the service of my King and Country requires it should be put to the test, that I am not deficient in either bravery or conduct, willingly and gallantly, to vindicate the former, or perform my duty in the support of the latter.

"ABRAHAM DE PEYSTER,

"Savannah, *Sept. 10th, 1781*."

"Captain K. A. Regiment.

TO THE PUBLIC.

"Reading the *London Political Magazine* the other day, I find that some person, entirely a stranger to the nature of the capture of the 7th of October, 1780, at *King's Mountain*, has inserted the most *egregious falsehoods that a malicious heart could dictate*, respecting Captain DE PEYSTER'S conduct on that day. As an officer of the division which Captain DE PEYSTER commanded in the engagement, I am free to declare that no officer, agreeable to my opinion (as well as to that of every other officer then on the spot), could have acted with more spirit or done more than that gentleman did : and the reports of the *Political Magazine* respecting Captain DE PEYSTER, I take upon myself to declare altogether destitute of truth.

"ANTHONY ALLAIRE, Lieutenant,
"Loyal American Regiment,"
"Charleston, August 4th, 1781."

Copied and forwarded from the British Museum (Department of Manuscripts), London, England, 8th December, 1881, through the courtesy of E. MAUNDE THOMPSON, Esq., to *Hon.* ISAAC N. ARNOLD, *President of the Chicago Historical Society*, Chicago, Illinois, for General de Peyster to insert in his publication on the Battle of King's Mountain.

www.ingramcontent.com/pod-product-compliance
Lightning Source LLC
Chambersburg PA
CBHW020255170426
43202CB00008B/384